THE WINE BIBBER'S BIBLE

a practical guide to selecting and enjoying wines

THE WINE BIBBER'S BIBLE

BY JAMES NORWOOD PRATT

with the collaboration of
JACQUES de CASO

and an essay by
CHARLES BAUDELAIRE

drawings by
SARA RAFFETTO

published by
101 PRODUCTIONS
San Francisco

ACKNOWLEDGEMENTS

Excerpts have been quoted from
the following books with the
generous permission of their publishers.

Hilaire Belloc. *Advice.*
Harvill Press, London.
Copyright © 1960 Bridget Grant.

Creighton Churchill. *The World of Wines.*
The Macmillan Company, New York.
Copyright © 1963, 1964 Creighton Churchill.

Hugh Johnson. *Wine.*
Simon and Schuster, New York;
Thomas Nelson and Sons, London.
Copyright © 1966 Hugh Johnson.

Idwal Jones. *Vines in the Sun.*
William Morrow and Company, New York.
Copyright © 1949 Idwal Jones.

John Melville. *Guide to California Wines.*
Nourse Publishing, San Carlos.
Copyright © 1955, 1960 John Melville.
Third Edition, revised by Jefferson Morgan;
copyright © 1968 Jefferson Morgan.

George Saintsbury. *Notes on a Cellarbook.*
St. Martin's Press, New York;
The Macmillan Company of Canada;
The Macmillan Company of London.
Copyright © 1933 The Macmillan Company.

Frank Schoonmaker and Tom Marvel.
The Complete Wine Book.
Simon and Schuster, New York.
Copyright © 1934.

Allan Sichel et al. *A Guide to Good Wine.*
Copyright © 1952 W & R Chambers, Ltd.,
London and Edinburgh;
Copyright © 1970 Murrays Sales and
Service Company, Publishers, London.

Illuminated initials designed and executed by John Immel.
Maps designed and executed by John C. W. Carroll.

Third printing, November, 1972

CONTENTS

TO JOHN, SUSAN, ROSALYN & GETTYS

Vinum tu facies bonum bibendo

AN ESSAY ON WINE
By Charles Baudelaire

Il faut être toujours ivre. – C.B.

8

great celebrity who was also a great fool—roles that often go hand in hand, it appears, as I shall more than once have the grievous pleasure of showing—such a man, I say, in a book about cuisine written from the twin viewpoints of health and pleasure dared to write the following under the entry "wine": "The Patriarch Noah is said to be the inventor of wine. It is a liquor made from the fruit of the vine."

And after that? After that, nothing: that's all. Leaf through the volume at will, turn the sense of it around, read it backwards, upside down, right to left and left to right, you will not find anything else on wine in *The Physiology of Taste* by the very illustrious and very respected Brillat-Savarin. "The Patriarch Noah . . ." and "It is a liquor . . . ."*

Imagine that an inhabitant of the moon or some distant planet, traveling in our world and wearied by the long stages of his journey, wants to wet his whistle and warm his stomach. He means to familiarize himself with our world's pleasures and customs. He has vaguely heard mention made of

*On a night made memorable by an excellent Oregon White Riesling, our host and friend Lew Baer brought to our attention one other mention of wine in Brillat-Savarin which Baudelaire apparently overlooked.

"Wine is the king of liquids and carries the exhaltation of the palate to the furthest degree. When one drinks, as long as the wine is retained in the mouth one has an agreeable but not complete perception of its flavor. It is only at the moment when one ceases to swallow that one can really taste, appraise and appreciate the aroma peculiar to each kind of wine. A short interval is necessary before the gourmet can pronounce 'it is good,' 'passable' or 'bad'; 'By Jove, it's Chambertin!' or 'Good Lord, it's Suresnes!' "

delicious liquors from which citizens of this globe obtain at will courage and lightheartedness. To choose one intelligently, the moon dweller opens that oracle of taste, the well-known and infallible Brillat-Savarin, and under the entry "Wine" he finds this priceless information: "The Patriarch Noah . . ." and "It is a liquor . . . ." Doesn't that hit the nail on the head! It says it all. After reading this no one could lack a clear and correct idea of all wines, their different qualities, their limitations and their potency in the stomach and the brain.

Ah, dear friends, don't read Brillat-Savarin! "Those He cherishes God preserves from useless reading." Such is the first maxim in a little book by Lavater, a philosopher who loved mankind more than all the magistrates of the world, ancient and modern. They have never christened a pastry with the name Lavater. The memory of that angelic man will be alive nevertheless among Christians when *les braves bourgeois* themselves shall have forgotten the little cake named after Brillat-Savarin—a sort of tasteless brioche, the least shortcoming of which is that it furnishes a pretext for disgorging innanely pedantic maxims culled from the famous masterpiece.

What if a new edition of this fake masterpiece dares challenge the good sense of modern man—will you bestow benefit upon indifference? Will you exchange good for bad and buy yourself a copy? Melancholy drinkers, joyful drinkers, all you who look for remembrance or forgetfulness in wine, never finding as much as you seek; and you who look at the world through the bottom of a bottle, drinkers forgotten and misunderstood—I ask you.

Opening the divine Hoffmann's *Kreisleriana,* I read there a curious prescription. The conscientious composer ought to make use of wine from Champagne in composing a comic opera. He will find in it the light, relaxed gaiety that the genre calls for. Religious music demands wine from the Rhine or Jurançon. There, as in the depths of profound thoughts, one finds an intoxicating poignancy. Heroic music, on the other hand, requires wine from Burgundy. It has the intense ardor and drive of patriotism. Now this says something, and besides a drinker's impassioned feelings, I find in this an impartiality that does the greatest honor to a German.

Hoffmann had drawn up a peculiar psychological barometer which he intended to indicate the different temperatures and atmospheric phenomena of his soul. On it one finds such divisions as these:

"Lightly ironic spirit tempered with indulgence.

Spirit of solitude with profound self-contentment.

Musical gaiety.

Musical enthusiasm.

A musical tempest.

Cynical gaiety I find unbearable.

Aspiration of escaping my ego.

Overwhelming awareness of reality.

Fusion of my being with nature."

The gradations of Hoffmann's psychological barometer, it goes without saying, follow the order in which these states occur, as those of ordinary barometers do. It appears to me that there is an obvious kinship between this barometer and the exposition of the musical qualities of wines.

Hoffmann was just beginning to make money at the time of his death. Fortune was smiling upon him. Like our great and dear Balzac, he saw the glow of the Aurora Borealis of his earliest expectations only in his last years. In this period editors were competing for his tales for their journals. Hoping to get into his good graces, they would add to the money they sent him a case of French wines.

Profound joys of wine, who has not known you? Whoever has had a remorse to appease, a memory to evoke, a grief to drown, a castle in Spain to build—in short every one has invoked you, mysterious god secreted in the fibers of the vine. How great are the pageants of wine, lit up by sunlight from within. How real and how burning is the second youth that man finds in it. But how threatening also, its raptures, its enervating enchantments. Tell me, however, in your your soul and conscience—judges, legislators, citizens, all you whom happiness has tamed and whose fortunes painlessly provide morals and good health, tell me—which of you will summon the pitiless courage to condemn the man who soaks up genius?

In any case wine is not always that terrible adversary sure of its victory and sworn to show neither pity nor mercy. For wine is just like man: no one can say how much respect and how much contempt it deserves, how much love and hate. Nor shall we ever know how many high deeds or monstrosities it is capable of. Let us therefore be no crueler towards wine than towards ourselves; let us treat it as an equal.

I sometimes think I hear wine talking. It speaks with its soul, with that spiritual voice which is only heard by the spirit: "Man, my beloved, from within my prison of glass locked with cork I yearn to sing you a song full of brotherhood, a song full of joy and light and expectation. I am not ungrateful; I know I owe this life to you. I know it has cost you labor with the sun beating down on your shoulders. You have given me life, and I shall recompense you. Generously shall I repay my debt, for I experience an enormous joy when I tumble down a work-parched throat. An honest man's chest is a resting place that pleases me much more than these melancholy and unfeeling cellars. It is a joyous tomb where I fulfill my destiny with enthusiasm. I create a prodigious flurry in the worker's stomach and from there by invisible staircases I climb to his brain where I perform my supreme dance. Do you hear stirring and re-echoing mighty choruses of ancient times in me, songs of love and of glory? I am the soul of your homeland, part troubadour and part soldier. The hope of Sundays am I. Work makes for prosperous weekdays, wine for happy Sundays. With your sleeves rolled up and your elbows on the family table, you will glory in me proudly and you will be truly content.

I will light up the eyes of your aged wife, the old partaker of your daily regrets and of your oldest expectations. I shall soften her gaze and place deep in her pupil the bright light of her youth. And your dear little boy, the poor little donkey, all pale and already harnessed to his labors like a drayhorse, I will restore to that lovely color he had in his cradle. For this new athlete in life shall I serve as the oil that strengthened the muscles of ancient contestants.

Like a botanical ambrosia I will plunge into the depths of your chest. I will be the grain sowed in the painfully plowed furrow. Our intimate reunion will create poetry. Together we two will make a god and fly toward infinity like birds, butterflies, gossamers, perfumes and all winged creatures."

This is what the wine sings in its mysterious language. Woe to him whose egoistic heart, closed to the griefs of his brother, has never heard this song. I have often thought that if Jesus Christ were to appear as a defendant today, the prosecutor would consider his case all the more serious because he has a previous conviction. Wine is likewise a recidivist and repeats its offenses every day. Day in and day out, it repeats its benefactions. No doubt this accounts for the moralists' fury against it. When I say moralist I mean our pseudo-moralistic Pharisees.

14

But here is something altogether different. Let us step a little lower down. Let us contemplate one of those mysterious beings who lives, so to speak, on the garbage of great cities. A huge number of people follow peculiar trades. I have sometimes thought with terror how there must be trades that bring no joy, work empty of pleasure offering unrelieved effort and pains nobody pays for. I was wrong. Here is a man charged with collecting the débris of one day in the life of the capital. Everything the great city has thrown away, all that it lost, discarded and broke he sorts and collects. He browses the archives of debauch, the junkheap of refuse. He makes a selection, an intelligent choice. Like a miser with his treasure, he assembles the cast-offs which can be fed back to the divinity of Industry and become objects of usefulness or pleasure. It is he beneath the somber light of gas jets tortured by the nighttime winds, who climbs one of those long, twisting streets lined with little households up the Mount Ste. Geneviève. He wears a garment which is woven of straw and has his number, seven, on it. He comes along, nodding and stumbling on the paving stones just like young poets who spend their days wandering and looking for rhymes. He talks to himself, his soul revolving in the cold and dark night air. His monologue is splendid: the most lyrical of tragedies would suffer by comparison. "Forward march. Staff! Division! Army!" Exactly like Buonaparte in agony on Ste. Helena! His number seven seems to become an iron scepter and his straw-woven covering an imperial robe. Now he is complimenting his army. It's been a hot day, but the battle is won. He rides under arches of triumph on horseback. His heart is high. He listens with delight to the acclamations of an enthusiastic world. Soon he's going to dictate a code of law superior to all codes known. He solemnly swears to make his people happy. Misery and vice have vanished from the world!

His back and hips, however, are irritated beneath the weight of his collection basket. He is plagued by domestic misfortune. He is worn out by forty years of work and his rounds. Age torments him. But wine, like another River Pactolus*, rolls bits of intellectual gold along a bed of languishing humanity. It rules, like good kings, by virtue of its achievements; the throats of its subjects are full of its praises.

Upon our terrestrial globe exists an innumerable and nameless throng, and not even sleep is enough to obliterate their miseries. Wine composes songs and poems for them.

No doubt many people will find me too indulgent. "You make drunkenness seem innocent. You idealize profligacy." I admit that I lack the courage to add up griefs before counting benefits. But anyway I've said that wine is analogous to man, and I consider the crimes of both of them equal to their virtues. Can I do any better? I have, besides, one other thought. If wine should disappear from among the things man makes, I believe it would leave in the health and intellect of the planet a void, an absence and a flaw far more horrendous than all the excess and deviation for which it gets blamed. Is it unreasonable to think that people who never, either casually or habitually, drink wine are imbeciles or else hypocrites? I consider imbeciles those who know neither man nor nature, artists who repudiate the traditions of their art, or workers who scoff at tools. Those gourmandisers who are ashamed of themselves and the childish boasters of sobriety who drink in secret and keep their wine hidden I call hypocrites. A man with a secret to hide from his fellow men is he who drinks only water.

*Ancient name for a small river in Lydia (modern Turkey) famous for the quantities of gold in its stream bed. The Lydian King Midas was said to have bathed in this river during the time everything he touched turned to gold.

To cite an example: at an exhibition of paintings some years ago, the mob of imbeciles made a great to-do over a painting which was polished, waxed and varnished like some industrial product. It was the absolute antithesis of art. It was to the kitchen-scene Drolling* painted, what madness is to stupidity, or what a slave is in comparison with a mere imitator. In this microscopic painting one beheld flies flying. This monstrous object attracted me like every one else; anything horrible attracts us irresistibly and I felt ashamed of my weakness in yielding to it. Eventually I perceived that a philosophical curiosity was building up in me against my wishes, an immense desire to know what the moral character of the man who had given birth to so criminal an extravagance could be. I bet myself that he had to be an essentially immoral man. I had information sought out and it confirmed my original instinct and gave me the gratification of winning this psychological bet. I learned that the monster rose regularly before dawn, that he had ruined his housemaid, and that *he only drank milk.*

One or two more stories and we shall dogmatize. One day I saw a big gathering on the sidewalk. I managed to look over the shoulders of the throng, and this is what I beheld. A man stretched out on the ground on his back, his open eyes staring at the sky; another man standing in front of him, gesturing and speaking only in signs; the man on the ground only answering with his eyes, and both of them apparently animated by the greatest good-will. To the prone man the gestures of the one standing conveyed: "Come now, come on! Happiness is only two steps thataway. Let's make it on down to the corner of the street. The banks of chagrin are still in sight;

*Martin Drolling (1752-1817) French painter, "L'Intérieur d'une Cuisine," his master-piece, now hangs in the Louvre.

we're not in the open sea of reverie yet. *Courage, mon ami.* Let's go! Tell your legs to obey your thoughts."

All this he conveyed by swayings and graceful dance steps. The other had no doubt reached the open sea (in fact he was navigating the gutter), for his beatific smile answered: "Leave your friend in peace. The bank of chagrin is well enough hidden behind those kindly clouds. I have nothing more to ask of the sea of reverie." I even believe I heard a vague sentence, or rather a sigh vaguely formulated in words leave his lips: "Try to be reason-able." Here is the height of the sublime. But drunkenness knows the hyper-sublime, as you shall see. The ever indulgent friend went to the cabaret by himself; he returned with a rope in his hand. No doubt he was unable to endure the thought of sailing and chasing after happiness all alone. He came looking for his friend with a vehicle. The vehicle was the rope. This vehicle he passed around his hips. His friend lying full length smiled, for doubtless he grasped this motherly intention. The other tied a knot and then like a docile and understanding horse, he set out to carry his friend to their rendezvous with happiness. The man who was carried, or dragged rather, polishing the pavement with his back, went on smiling his ineffable smile. The crowd stood there stupefied, for whatever surpasses man's capacity for poetry causes more astonishment than compassion.

Once there was a man, a Spaniard who played the guitar and travelled with Paganini for a long time. This was before the period of Paganini's great official recognition.

The two of them led the great vagabond life of gypsies, of strolling players, people without family or homeland. This pair, the violin and the guitar, gave concerts wherever they went. In this way they wandered through many countries for a long time. My Spaniard was so talented that he could say like Orpheus, "I rule over nature." Wherever he went, striking his chords and making the strings pop harmoniously under his thumb, he was sure to have a crowd following him. A person in possession of such a secret never starves to death. They followed him like Jesus Christ. Who could refuse a meal and hospitality to a man or genius or sorcerer who has touched your soul and made it sing its loveliest, obscurest, least known and most mysterious airs? I have been assured that this man easily obtained continuous sounds from an instrument which produces sounds in succession only. Paganini held the purse, which should surprise no one. He administered their mutual funds, and the money traveled on the person of the administrator. He kept it in different places, in his boots today and tomorrow between his shirt tails. When the guitarist, who was quite a drinker, would ask how their finances stood, Paganini would tell him that nothing or practically nothing was left. Paganini was like some old people who always live in terror of going without. The Spaniard believed or pretended to believe him, and fixing his eyes on the horizon of the road, would go on strumming and fretting his inseparable companion. Paganini walked on the other side of the road from him. This was done by mutual agreement so that neither would annoy the other. Each could thus study and work while walking along.

When they reached some place that presented a chance of income one of the two would play a composition of his own while beside him the other would improvise a variation, accompaniment or background. How much pleasure and poetry they found in this troubadour's life, no one will ever know. I do not know why but they separated; from then on, the Spaniard traveled alone. One evening, he found himself in a little town in the Jura mountains. He posted notices announcing a concert in a room at the town hall. The concert, a recital, consisted of the one guitar. By playing in

certain cafés he had made himself known and there were some music lovers in the town who had been struck by his strange talent. Many people showed up.

Now in a spot beside the town cemetery, my Spaniard had dug up another Spaniard from his neck of the woods. He was a sort of sepulchral contractor by trade, a marble cutter who made tombstones. Like all the people in the funereal trades he drank a good deal. The bottle and the native land these two had in common kept them together and the musician would not leave the marble cutter. On the day of the concert, and at the very hour it was to begin, they were together still, but where? That was the question. They were hunted through all the cabarets and all the cafés in the town. The two were eventually unearthed in a dive that defies description, both of them perfectly drunk. The scenes that followed were worthy of Kean or Frédérick*.

The Spaniard finally agreed to go play. Then he suddenly had an idea; "You play with me," he said to his friend. The friend refused. He had a violin, but he was the clumsiest of fiddlers. "Either you play or else I will not." Neither entreaties nor good reasons had any effect; the die was cast. There they were then, on the platform in front of the cream of the local society. "Fetch some wine," said the Spaniard. The maker of tombstones, who was known to all but certainly not as a musician, was too drunk to be embarrassed. They did not even take the trouble to uncork the bottles once

*Antoine-Louis-Prosper Frédérick-Lemaître (1800-1876) a French actor famous for his eloquence, powerful emoting and epic clowning.
*Edmund Kean (1787-1833) great English actor especially noted for his performances in Shakespearean roles.

the wine appeared. Showing no manners at all, my ruffianly pair guillotined their bottles with a knife. Imagine the effect on a provincial audience dressed up in its Sunday-best! The ladies withdrew. Many perfectly scandalized people walked out on these two inebriates who appeared to be half crazy. But those who were not so straight that they were bereft of all curiosity and who had nerve enough to stay never regretted it. "Begin," the guitarist told the marble worker. Words could not describe the kind of sound that drunken violin emitted: a delirious Bacchus carving stone with a saw! What was he playing or trying to play? That mattered little once the music began.

A descant, energetic yet suave, capricious but still all of a piece, all at once enveloped, cloaked, suffocated and extinguished the raucous noise. The guitar sang out so that the violin was no longer heard. It was, however, the very same melody, the wine-laden melody the marble cutter had embarked on. The guitar was enormously sonorous in expressing itself. It chit-chatted, it sang, it declaimed with fearful verve and with an authority and purity such as is never heard in speech. The guitar improvised a variation on the blind violin's theme. She let herself be guided by it, and splendidly and maternally she clothed the raw nudity of its sounds. My reader will understand why all this defies description. A reliable eye-witness told me the story. The public was more intoxicated than the performers by the end. My Spaniard was feted, complimented, greeted with immense enthusiasm. But the temperament of the people in that neck of the woods must have displeased him for that was the only occasion he ever consented to play. Where is he now? What sun witnessed his last daydreams? What soil covered his cosmopolitan corpse? What ditch sheltered his agony?

Where do the intoxicating fragrances of vanished flowers go? Where are the fairyland colors created by setting suns in years gone by?

I doubt that you have learned anything very new from all this. Wine is known to every one and it is loved by all. Some day we shall see a truly philosophical doctor, a phenomenon barely imaginable today. He will be able to make a penetrating study of wine, a sort of duplex psychology whose two facets are wine and man. He will explain how and why certain beverages possess the power of expanding beyond measure the personality of the thinking being and of creating a third person, so to speak. For this is a mystical operation in which man in his natural condition and wine, the animal god and the vegetable god, play the roles of the Father and the Son in the Trinity. The Holy Spirit which they engender is the superior man whose existence requires the two of them combined.

Some individuals find the stimulating effects of wine so powerful that their limbs become stronger and their hearing exceedingly fine. I knew a person whose weakened eyesight recovered all its old power to perceive when he was drinking. Wine transformed the mole into an eagle.

An old and unknown author has said "Nothing equals the pleasure of the man who drinks unless it is the joy of the wine at being drunk." The role wine plays in the life of mankind is truly an intimate one; so intimate that I should not be surprised at certain reasonable minds being seduced into a pantheistic attitude and attributing to it a kind of personality. Wine and man seem to me two friendly rivals, ceaselessly contending and ceaselessly reconciled one with the other. The vanquished always embraces the conqueror.

TRANSLATORS' NOTE

This essay is part of a book-length study on the effects of drugs entitled *Les Paradis Artificiels* which was first published *in toto* in 1860 by Baudelaire's friend Poulet-Malassis. The text used for this translation follows the 1869 edition. This essay, *"Du Vin et du Haschisch Comparé comme Moyen de Multiplication de l'Individualité,"* had first appeared in 1851 in the journal *Messager de l'Assemblée*. The discrepancies between different editions are few and minor. Except for the omission of the last eighteen lines which form the bridge to Baudelaire's treatment of hashish, we have translated the wine section of the essay without deletions. Long a classic of French literature, *Les Paradis Artificiels* has only recently been rendered into English for the first time in its entirety by Ellen Fox and has been published under the title *Artificial Paradises* by the New York firm of Herder and Herder in 1971.

J.N.P.
J. de C.

WINE TALK
What are you trying to tell me?

Some use wine for profit, some to make them merry withal, and some for pleasure, and some for all these purposes. Wine doth not only nourish, but maketh the meats to go well down, and stirreth up the natural heat and increaseth it . . . . But if a man will use it wisely, it will digest or distribute the nourishment, increase the blood and nourish; it will also make the mind both gentler and bolder.

—William Turner, from the first book on wines in English

t is said of the French diplomat Talleyrand that he only once reproached a guest for not showing the proper respect due some particularly fine vintage. "I would willingly do so if only you would show me how, sire," his embarassed table companion replied. "First you must hold your glass to the light and swirl the wine slowly to study its color." "Yes?" "Then you bring the glass to your nose to breathe the wine's bouquet." "And then?" "And then, young man, you set your glass down and you talk about it."

Talking about wine has ever been one of the many pleasures this ancient and divine drink affords those who love it. That is why this book about wine is being written.

Of all the curious actions of which our mere bodies are capable, the two that most readily fire the imagination are making love and drinking wine. Talking about wine can sometimes make us feel the way we did as adolescents discussing sex—unwilling to seem totally ignorant but hesitant to express ourselves freely lest we discover ourselves in the company of some-one who "knows all about it." Nobody does, of course, and eventually we realize why nobody ever could: some subjects are inexhaustible. Such animals as the wine "expert" do exist, however, and we shall never know as much as those makers, merchants and tasters who spend all their time with wine. They are experts, and the expertise goes along with their profession. But we amateurs need offer no apology for our opinions so long as we are worthy of that noble name. Obscured though its basic meaning has become in present English usage, the word "amateur" is descended from the Latin

experts and amateurs

verb *amo,* "I love." The wine expert must make wine his livelihood, but the "amateur" is a lover of wine for its own sake.

Webster's notwithstanding, the wine connoisseur does not need to be a wine expert, and neither does the wine bibber need to be a connoisseur. We are all perfectly competent to judge what pleases us and what does not in *connoisseurship* entertainment, food and drink. After all, your taste is as uniquely your own as your fingerprints are. If you have drunk enough wine to discover a preference for some—and perhaps a distaste for others—you are already in the ranks of the world's wine bibbers. The rightful object of all learning is enjoyment, and one gradually learns to distinguish different degrees of pleasure. To know what you mean when you call one movie or steak "good" and another "great" is to pass a critical judgment based on past experience and this is the essence of connoisseurship. It's not a word to attach too much importance to. As you unconsciously absorb knowledge, make comparisons and discover circumstances in which you prefer this wine to that over the years, you become by degrees a connoisseur. If your taste continues to develop, you probably also raise your standards of taste and appreciation. In time your friends may consider that your love of wine has led you to adopt strange, esoteric practices and to mutter mystic formulae while you drink. You must try to explain that like any other esthetic creation, like poetry, painting, music or dance, the more you come to know about wine, the more you find in it to enjoy. Tell them about Talleyrand.

M. de Talleyrand—if it was really he and not another responsible for our anecdote—was no crackpot. He was an Experienced Connoisseur showing *wine slang* a novice how to make the most of one of the gods' greatest gifts. Terms like "bouquet" are just part of the slang of wine lore. In every specialized thing we do, be it sewing, fishing or ping pong, there are specialized terms. Wine makers and wine drinkers have theirs too.

Now some unfortunates drink labels instead of wine. They always notice a wine's faults before finding any virtues in it, and they are always especially careful to lace their comments liberally with wine slang to impress you. James Thurber epitomized this dread disorder, wine snobbery, in his memorable cartoon, "It's a naive domestic Burgundy without any breeding, but I think you'll be amused by its presumption."

Such pretentious people are not hard to recognize, and their misuse of wine slang should not blind us to its value. A word like "breeding" need not be affectation; it actually has a fairly definite meaning. A good Chateauneuf-du-Pape may boast a dozen excellent qualities, not the least of which is its moderate price. Taste it, however, after a Margaux or a first-rate Cabernet Sauvignon and it is not difficult to sense that these wines are clothed in a certain unaggressive elegance to which the forthright Rhône makes no claim. The word "breeding" expresses it exactly. Tell your friends to beware of over-hasty headshaking if they hear you using such language. Why should the man who tells you in detail about his customized automobile expect rapt attention and yet consider you a suspicious character should you fondly recollect your last Lafite-Rothschild? The car's body cannot compare with the Claret's, and obsolescence is built into the one as longevity is built into the other. Ah well, perhaps it's sometimes better to be silent; you don't want to come on like your neighbor with his comparative history of the major-league shortstops over the past twenty seasons.

"And Noah began to be an husbandman, and he planted a vineyard . . . ." Presumably he had opportunity to compare his own product with that of other wineries, for *Genesis* later assures us that " . . . Noah lived

the communication question

29

after the Flood three hundred and fifty years." The name by which he called the gift of the grape probably sounded much like our own word "wine." At

least the Hittites, whose language was dominant in the Mount Ararat neighborhood as early as 1500 B.C. referred to it in their hieroglyphic script as *uin-*. *Woi-ne-wei* occurs as the word for wine merchant in Mycenean Greek; in Archaic Greek wine is *woinos,* which loses its W to become *oinos* in classical times. The W sound was retained in the Etruscan and Latin derivative *vinum* (V sounding like W in Latin) and its offshoots, *vino, vin, wein,* and *wine.* The Hittite term found its way into other neighboring languages—*gini* in Armenian and *gvino* in Georgian—and was adopted into the Semitic tongues also, becoming in Hebrew *vayin* and remaining as *wa-yn* in Arabic today. (We are indebted to Professor Charles Seltman's *Wine in the Ancient World* for this fascinating piece of *viniana.*) If music is the international language, wine, historically, has been the international word.

"De gustibus non disputandum est," wrote Horace. "Taste is nothing to argue over." The poet's sagacious suggestion grates against human nature, particularly the nature of the world's wine lovers who continue to honor it

only in the breach. We may be sure that men were disputing the imagined merits of various wines in this country long before they produced America's first wine in 1564 from grapes that were growing wild in Florida. Now wines made from native American grapes are so different from any others that comparisons would be absurd. Their devotees are content to quote Longfellow's

> But Catawba Wine
> Has a taste more divine,
> More dulcet, delicious, and dreamy . . . .

and thus justified, to ignore, almost or utterly, all other wines whatsoever.

Native American grapes belong to the *labrusca* family and are mainly raised in the Eastern part of the United States. This Eastern wine industry is centered in New York and Ohio, but has vineyards in the South and Midwest and elsewhere.

The completely separate Californian industry supplies some 75 to 80 percent of our domestic wines. Californian and European wines are blood relatives, so to speak, for both come from grapes belonging to the *vinifera* or "winebearer" family. The California progeny of the European varieties are brought up under the very different conditions of the nine growing regions in that state and produce wines with a character all their own, reminiscent but not imitative of European. The time is long past when Californians need feel the least defensive about the quality of their wines. Quoth, for one, Mr. Hugh Johnson, one of our most eminent authorities on all matters vinous: "Of all the vineyards of the New World, California is the one which has suffered most discouragement ... and yet the one which makes the best wine. Of the other new lands of the vine you can say that many of their wines are good and some fine. Of California you can say that many of her wines are fine and some great."

California wines

Where a vine is planted is the most important single factor determining the quality of the wine it produces and the specific *goût de terroir* or taste of ground it has. If one insists upon making comparisons, it is possible, even instructive, to compare California's Rieslings with the wines of the Rhine, Cabernet Sauvignon with Bordeaux, and so forth—so long as you don't expect one to be a copy of the other. Now many people whose palates are habituated to Old World wine flavors set up European wines, probably unconsciously, as a standard against which they measure all others. They tend to class these others as good or bad in direct proportion to the degree

"terroir"

comparisons

to which they imitate European wines. For example, Creighton Churchill, Esq. writes of French sparkling Burgundy: "The only thing to recommend it, as opposed to its California or New York State cousins, is that it is at least made of Old World grapes on Old World soil—and thus its taste carries a certain hint of Old World *'terroir'*." We find very little to recommend any sparkling Burgundy but then . . . *"De gustibus non disputandum est."*

talking about wine

    We have strayed from our topic. M. de Talleyrand would not have us set our glasses down and declare allegiance to one or another wine-producing region, which would be folly in any case. No, you talk about the wine before you because it is the nature of wine to make one talk. It is also interesting because our sensations are so personal and subjective. A wine he considers "light" you may find as full of body as Homer. Furthermore, a fine wine has such a complex character that different tasters may be struck more by one element than by another, depending upon what each is most sensitive to. There's truth in the old proverb "In water you see your own face, in wine the heart of another." To talk about what you feel, what you discover and enjoy, is to reveal yourself and take another into your confidence. Wine loosens the tongue at the same time it maketh glad the heart. But to share, to compare and analyze the subtle, fleeting impressions a wine produces is not only to communicate with another but to discover for oneself what, exactly, those impressions are. The qualities and precise sensations we perceive must be crystallized into words or they are soon lost to us and easily forgotten. If you're called upon for an opinion of a wine you find mediocre or unpleasant, it is of course better not to talk than to give offense. You can always confine yourself to a laconic "interesting" and still be telling the truth. After all, it is interesting to taste wines one dislikes if only to know what not to buy for oneself.

*what wine
has to say*

But part of any pleasure comes from discussing it, and to characterize and compare sensations which exist in a realm where no word has ever entered, we are compelled to invent a language that draws upon vocabulary used in other fields and to speak in images and symbols. You may, if you like, free your fantasy and find in your wine the shavings of cherubs' wings, the glory of a tropic dawn, the red clouds of sunsets or fragments of lost epics by dead masters. If you pay attention to it, a good wine will always have something to tell you. What exactly it says no one can ever completely understand, of course, and that is wine's charm and its mystery. But bursts of lyricism are not always necessary to describe what you prefer in today's Burgundy to the one you drank last week. It's really no more difficult than telling someone why, say, you think *Satyricon* Fellini's greatest film. There are no authorities in matters of taste, and there's no danger of appearing ridiculous so long as your similes don't appear in print. To find André Simon calling a wine "a girl of fifteen coming in on tiptoes" on the cold printed page may well make us smile. But had we been there, glass in hand, to share that bottle with him, no doubt we should have known what he meant at once. No doubt, too, he would have wanted to hear what we thought of it.

ordinaire

Not all wines deserve discussion. The wines that serve as everyday drink may call for an "I like it" or "The wine is all right," and that's all there is to that. At least four-fifths and maybe more of the world's wine production is made to be consumed within a year of fermentation. This completely anonymous wine is what the French call *vin ordinaire*. Having no word for it in English, we've borrowed the French term and usually call it *ordinaire* ourselves. Most of our American *ordinaires* are generic wines—named, that is, after European prototypes which they are intended to resemble, more or less. (Varietal wines are those named after the grape variety from which they are made. More on this later.) *Ordinaire* is not always made by trolls and need not be repulsive to the palate—much of it is gulpable enough. It simply lacks any kind of character by which to distinguish one from another.

When we come to good wine we begin to have something to talk about. What do you mean when you say a dish is good? What makes a new song good? We must include here everything from just plain well made on upwards. Good wine is true to type and cannot be mistaken for anything except what it says it is. If it's labeled dry Sauterne and tastes no different from Chablis to you, you may be sure you're drinking *ordinaire*. Furthermore, good wine is sufficiently individualistic to be worth tasting with some attention. In other words, it's not just drinkable, it's interesting. Most of the California generic wines labeled as to county of origin fall into this category and a good deal of her varietal wine as well. Good covers the whole field between *ordinaire* and fine wines. Good wine is nothing to rave about, but it is something to be thankful for.

good

Fine wine, on the other hand, is a blessing. These are the bottles which may lack greatness, but are much more than merely good. It is safe to say that the acknowledged fine wines of North America come almost exclusively from Northern California. Fine wine can only be produced from certain grape varieties cultivated on ground that has the ideal chemical properties for that wine grape, the best exposure to the sun and just the right amount of rainfall, in addition to protection from winds and frosts. There are not too many of these places to be found on the globe. They produce wine that is not simply alive, it's lively. Whereas good wine may be interesting, fine wine is exciting. Every so often you discover a fine California generic wine like the Inglenook Chablis of 1966 we remember so fondly (along with a number of others), but the great majority of fine California

fine

wines are varietals. There will be more of it now that recent tax laws will allow winemakers and merchants to age their most promising reds longer. Those wines a producer takes greatest pride in almost always carry the highest allowable appellation—"produced and bottled by . . . ." (and sometimes "estate-bottled" just for good measure), and they often, though by no means invariably, bear a vintage date. But let's postpone a discussion of vintage until later. The only sure test of a wine's quality is the taste of the wine; there are fine wines that are not famous, and famous wines that are not fine.

great   No vineyard or district in the world invariably produces great wine, for great wine is a miracle, the rare result of a perfect collaboration between man and nature under perfect conditions. These are the Nureyevs of the world of wine. It is even more difficult to generalize about the quality of greatness in wines than to draw the line between the fine and the great. All great wines differ from one another, having only their nobility in common. Their respective virtues may be debated, but each wine in this, our smallest category, is superb and each unique. The aftertaste of a great wine is just as complex, harmonious and delightful as the first whiff of its bouquet, and everything it has to offer is equally perfect. The experience of great wine is something every wine bibber should enjoy at least once a lifetime, if only to find out what all the fuss is about. We have every confidence we shall retain in the hereafter a clear recollection of certain great wines it has been our good fortune to encounter this go-round. Alexandre Dumas said you should drink Montrachet, the white Burgundy, only on your knees with your hat off. That's the way a great wine makes you feel.

We would only add there should be some one to share the experience with, for it is painful to have to keep such pleasure to oneself.

WINE TASTING
How do you know it's any good?

It is true that taste can be educated. It is also true that taste can be perverted . . . . If any man gives you a wine you can't bear, don't say it is beastly . . . but don't say you like it. You are endangering your soul and the use of wine as well. Seek out some other wine good to your taste.

—Hilaire Belloc

asting requires intelligence of the body as well as the mind. The sense of hearing is the only one of the five recognized senses which does not come into play in wine tasting, and even here there are poets to protest the contrary. Baudelaire is by no means the only one who sometimes thought he heard the soul of wine singing. There are others, including even Englishmen like old W. E. "Invictus" Henley.

> The spirit of wine sang in my glass and
> I hastened with love to this odorous music,
> His flushed and magnificent song.

Who can be sure whether or not Henley means us to take him literally? Certainly we shall not insist that wines never sing to those who love them, but most of us know only the sound they make gurgling into our glasses. "The wine experience," so to speak, begins with our visual sensations: the first thing that strikes us about a wine is its color. Red, rosé, *sight* white, each with its infinite range of shades. Red wines are often deep purple when new; some that have aged a long time turn the color of terra-cotta tiles. California rosés often show a distinct tinge of orange or may be almost red sometimes. Whites can be practically colorless, tending perhaps toward a very pale green; some show the glint of old gold. The French refer to a *"gown"* wine's color as its "gown." Like a log fire or a candle flame, the animation and beauty of a wine's color in the glass can induce long reveries if you let it. Experience alone teaches what color characteristics are more or less appropriate to the different types of wine.

Lifting the glass by its stem and looking through it at a source of light, whether simply the whiteness of the tablecloth or an electric light or whatever, enables you to perceive the wine's brilliancy, that is to say, its clarity. Most commercial wines are now filtered before shipment and should reach the consumer in a brilliant condition. But perhaps the clarity is imperfect, perhaps the "gown" seems a little dulled or there are even a few

sediment little "fishes" floating about. This is not a sign of negligence on the part of the bottler nor does it mean there's anything wrong with the wine. In fact, some knowledgeable wine lovers will not buy an old red which has no sediment in the bottle. When it exists it is a simple matter to pour the wine into a new bottle after the sediment has been allowed to settle, taking care in your handling and uncorking of the bottle not to stir it up again. But whether you decant or just pour carefully, the object is to increase your visual pleasure. Do not worry if a little sediment slips into your glass—it is not dirt and, being usually odorless and tasteless, will not pollute the wine's taste. At most you may feel something like a little dust on the tongue. It is not serious. Allow the wine to sit still a few moments in the glass and even this can be avoided—unless you down it in a gulp like medicine.

"legs" There is another element that can be revealed to the sight if one wants to look at the "legs" of the wine in his glass. When the glass is twirled and the wine then comes to rest again, the thin film of wine covering the wall of the glass forms into heavy transparent tears which slowly trickle down the curve of the crystal and leave behind them long trails that French wine tasters call the "legs" of the wine. There's a knack involved in swirling the wine in the glass without sloshing any out of it. Such a catastrophe can be avoided if the glass is half full or less and the aspiring leg watcher has practiced his twirl. The legs are the signs of a wine's richness. You can

deduce the degree of maturity, of "fatness" and unctuousness to come according to whether the legs are plentiful and dense or few and spaced out. Not all wines have legs to show, but with some, shorter legs follow the first ones and the glass will weep unendingly.

While the wine has been delighting the eye it has had time to breathe; now the nose can enjoy the splendors it has to offer. Authorities on the subject claim the human olfactory sense can distinguish between four-thousand and ten-thousand different odors. The odors of the grapes from which the wine was made are called "aromas." Thus any Pinot Chardonnay should have the characteristic Pinot Chardonnay aroma, and with a little practice you can learn to recognize it. The aroma is the part of the smell that you can expect. There are also odors that come from the processing or aging of the wine, and these constitute its bouquet. Many factors may result in widely different bouquets among several brands of the same wine. It takes time for a wine to develop bouquet, and you can never predict precisely what it will be like. Of course cheap wines will often smell so bad that it's pretentious to speak of aroma or bouquet at all—"fumes" is more like it.

smell

aroma and bouquet

Perfumes are heavier than air and will therefore collect in the top of the glass; filling the glass to the brim merely wastes the wine's delectable fragrance. Just sniff the wine to begin with and see if you can smell anything. Exhale completely to free your nostrils of the odor, and go back for another sniff. Pay attention to your sensations and you will probably discover something new that you missed at first. If the wine is good, there is a haunting compound of clean, fresh smells all bound together by a firm sweetness. No water drinker can imagine how many different sweetnesses there can be!

Now that you have made the acquaintance of this complex odor, it is time to get to know it well. Stick your nose into the glass and inhale very slowly and steadily. What now fills your head cannot be described as anything but a bouquet—a combination of all the perfumes in their full force. Very few wines are as wonderful as their smell, so linger over it as long as you like. Return to the bouquet again and again as you drink to see how it develops with increasing warmth and oxidation. If the wine is served chilled, *"frozen" bouquet* the bouquet may be "frozen" until the wine has warmed enough to release it. Dry whites and rosés, indeed most young wines, seem to have a certain fruity odor which can be attributed more to their youth and freshness than to the smell of the grape. If you are unable to detect much of a bouquet, it may be because the wine is too young or simply too "little," as they say, to have one. More rarely, the body of the wine may smother its odors, so that the nose has no way of suspecting the surprises in store for the palate.

It's just possible all this wine smelling may turn up some unpleasant discoveries; you must expect to encounter off-odors from time to time. *off-odors* Yeasty odors that should have disappeared during early aging sometimes don't. Or maybe the vintner was overenthusiastic in using sulphur-dioxide gas to prevent the development of harmful bacteria during the fermentation of the wine and it reeks of sulphur. This is most often noticed in whites and is a particularly nasty defect. Occasionally you may find a wine, particularly a red that's been bottled for a number of years, "corky." This is an *corkiness* indescribable but unmistakable moldiness that pervades both the odor and the taste of the wine, but unlike the previous defects, it's something you can put up with. Especially if it's the only wine in the house and it's raining out of doors. "Corkiness" is also the one quality that the greatest and least of wines sometimes have in common. The only other redeeming thing about it is that it is one of nature's unexplained mysteries—something to do with neurotic cork oaks, but nobody's sure quite what.

Now that you've listened to, looked at and smelled of the wine, it's finally time to take your first taste of it. But don't be hasty: the number of different sensations your tongue is about to undergo is in no way related to *taste* the amount of wine you can get into your mouth. The taste buds are not equally distributed in there. Most are on the tip and sides, with the remainder concentrated at the very back of the tongue. To begin with take only a sip, little more than a few drops of the wine, and roll it around to reach all these zones. It's as if the aroma of the wine becomes suddenly tangible as you hold this first sip in your mouth taking careful note of what the wine is trying to tell you. How dry is it? How acid? How astringent? Are all the various odor/flavors as harmonious in the mouth as they were in the *sipping* nose? You may want to take several little sips, concentrating on a different element each time.

Most wines reveal their deepest secret, the "central" taste standing out over the others, at first contact. But the flavor of wine is as complex as its chemistry, and if the wine is good its flavor will be many-layered, each component present individually and at the same time blended into a perfect whole. As with the bouquet, the taste of a wine oftentimes changes and develops as a bottle is consumed, and a wine one first judged to lack character may improve by being better known. Just as smells and tastes intermingle and sometimes merge altogether, the sensations we experience upon first tasting a wine are an almost imperceptible mingling of a number of different qualities. The challenge lies in perceiving these nuances. Wine-making is more an art than a science, and wine is made to be loved and not

simply drunk. To love it you have to appreciate its true character and for this, drinking is not enough; you must taste.

There are various tricks that tasters use to bring out the flavors in that first sip or two of wine. Some people hold a little on the tip of the tongue and suck air in over it. Others hold a like amount on the back of the tongue, open their mouths, and exhale over it. Either technique requires a little practice, and even then the chances are your gurgling will sound like faulty plumbing. The theory behind such carrying on is that aerating the wine *nella bocca* reveals any hidden aromas, and probably it does. If you find such a procedure has value, therapeutic or otherwise, there's no reason not to use it. But if it doesn't look good to you, or makes you self-conscious, you need not worry about missing anything as long as you taste attentively. What you do with the wine in your mouth is your business: the only affectation is to spit it out.

tasting tricks

The sense of touch also comes into play when you put anything in your mouth, and in evaluating or trying to describe the "feel" of a wine you must speak of its "body." The alcohol in the wine always produces a slightly burning sensation, though a "well-built" wine never feels hot. Body has to do with alcohol, therefore, but also with the wine's robustness or fullness of texture, the weight of the wine on your tongue. A rich red Pinot Noir or Barbera would seem somehow deficient if it were not obviously "full-bodied"–almost substantial enough to chew sometimes. A Gamay Beaujolais of similar consistency, on the other hand, would seem too thick, too "heavy-bodied"; such reds are meant to be lighter. Most white wines are even more light-bodied than any red, if you will permit an overly broad generalization. Looking at a wine's legs gives you a hint in advance as to how "fat" or how "thin" the body will prove to be. There is another trick of tasting

touch

"body"

that allows even finer discrimination, and this is to bring the wine into contact with the entire lining of the mouth and then press the tongue against the palate. You'll readily discover whether the wine has more the feel and consistency of water or of oil. We examine our sips in every way we can think of, interrogate our senses, and then the wine gets swallowed. The disappearance of the wine is not, however, the end of the pleasure we receive from it; there remains the aftertaste. Often this can be the most dazzling part of the whole experience, as you are suddenly left with an awareness of all *aftertaste* sorts of lingering fragrances that permeate the mouth and nose. You not only discover qualities that had hitherto gone unnoticed, but you are all at once reminded of each separate sensation leading up to this "finish," as the aftertaste is also sometimes called. A "little" wine, a "simple" wine, may have no more aftertaste than it has bouquet. Such a wine, that has not much to tell us and says it all at once, is said to "cut short its taste." With a fine wine the taste may stay on and on, as if to assure us our pleasures are no less real for being transitory.

We hasten to add, it takes much less time to do all these things than to read about them. However you go about it, the important thing is that you not simply fill your mouth and swallow, but rather pay attention to the wine the way you might taste a dish to see whether it needs more seasoning. And what makes this trouble worthwhile? A fair and philosophical question: Why? The satisfaction in wine tasting comes, not from finding fault with inferior wines, but from sharpening our senses, which is to say, cultivating our taste in the most basic meaning of that term. The idea is not just to enjoy but to make the most of that enjoyment. Too often we look without seeing, hear without listening, or—drink without tasting, surely the greatest insult you can offer a fine wine. It seems a waste indeed to pass up pleasures that can be ours in exchange for nothing more than attentiveness and concentration. These are faculties a taster exercises, and since anything one pays close attention to stays in the memory, he soon develops the ability to remember his sensations. M. André Malraux calls the works of art engraved in memory our "imaginary museums." Over the course of a lifetime we also stock our "imaginary wine cellars," for as Robert Louis Stevenson observed, "A bottle of good wine, like a good act, shines ever in the retrospect." Memory is the only paradise from which we cannot be driven, and wine creates memories for us. It makes us happy now and again twenty years from now by the memory of it. But we depend upon today's impressions for our memories tomorrow. These bottles, some plain and some precious, that lie asleep but still alive in the past, amply reward the taster for every respect he showed them.

"le musée imaginaire"

You don't have to be a fine connoisseur or greatly gifted or to have practiced tasting at your mother's knee in order to derive the greatest pleasures from tasting wines. The first wines one learns to enjoy are almost always ones that are easily recognized and understood. Sweetness always flatters the palate, and the tip of the tongue is the part most sensitive to it. Probably this explains why all of us know exactly how much sugar we like in our coffee and usually can tell whether that exact amount was exceeded even a little. Also for this reason the first wines people turn on to are often the flowery, slightly sweet whites like Green Hungarian and Chenin Blanc. In time one begins looking for greater subtlety and richness in wine, as in music or anything else. The sour-sensing taste buds lie along the edges of the tongue and the bitter-sensitive ones across the back. The progression in taste is generally said to follow this order also. One learns to enjoy and appreciate drier, tart white wines after the first not-so-dry ones and lastly the

sweet, sour, bitter

astringent, dry and faintly bitter reds. This at least is how the professors have it figured, though we really doubt that anything so logical can be true. Still it is a fact that it usually takes time to acquire new tastes and discover one's personal preferences. After all, the only taste we're born with is one for mother's milk and every other taste we have has been acquired sometime! *"acquired" tastes* Certainly it is only with time that the wine bibber becomes familiar with what to be sensitive to and learns what to look for in different wines. Although one's liking for wine can come with the first glass, you come to understand and appreciate it more and more with time and experience.

As in lovemaking, reading is a damned poor substitute for experience in the gentle art of tasting. It is one of those things you find out about for yourself. And despite its genteel associations, wine appreciation is no attainment; it's a pleasure and a game. If you wonder what we mean, get two similar wines and pour two glasses of one and a third glass of the other. You may number the glasses and shuffle them, or ask a friend to pour for you, so *the tasting game* long as you do not know which wine goes into which glass but have a way of keeping track. Then see if you can pick out the odd glass of wine. Your chances of guessing correctly are one in three, so the experiment should be repeated at least three times in a row. For best results rinse your mouth or chew a bit of bread and allow a few moments between wines. You will be surprised at how many differently delicious wines you can learn to recognize. You will remember the names easily once the tastes get fixed in your mind. It takes time for a taster to become familiar with what to look for and what to be sensitive to. A familiarity with wine aromas and flavors comes not so much through extensive as comparative sampling. Only by tasting one wine against another can we learn how to discriminate between them. The more we are able to discriminate, the better shall we be able to appreciate

the finer points of what is set before us. Nearly seven-and-a-half-billion gallons of wine are consumed every year in this world, and you can try out our tasting game with any of it. The better the wine is, of course, the more enjoyable the game becomes. Which is the better of any two similar wines? The one you prefer, certainly. And what's the difference between them? There isn't any if you can't find it.

Tis a pity wine should be so deleterious
For tea and coffee leave us much more serious.

—George Gordon Lord Byron

wine nuts and cellar books

You can be sure somebody's become a certified wine nut the day he starts to keep a cellar book or wine diary, though you can't be sure he'll admit to the seriousness of this symptom. Wine nuts are funny. All they actually have in those scrapbooks is dates and names of drinking companions, collages of raggedy old labels they steamed off bottles, stains and adjectives—delicate, racy, mild, noble, elegant, fruity, slender, harmonious, angular, unfinished, powerful, developed, dry, bitter, green, pure, earthy, ripe, masculine, soft, obtrusive, liquorous, stony, flattering, full, nutty, nervy, flat, strong, piquant, spicy, steely, characterless, fiery, flinty, blunt, . . . all sorts of words like that. Not, mind you, that your wine nut really trusts words! He knows that things are not all so comprehensible and expressible as we are led to believe, and most words come down to more or less happy misunderstandings.

WINE BUYING
What are you looking for?

The rapturous, wild, and ineffable pleasure of drinking at somebody else's expense . . .

—Henry S. Leigh

uying any kind of wine should be an occasion for directing dark thoughts at Washington and other government centers. Only the most expensive cost more per gallon to produce than milk. Wine costs what it costs because of a pyramid of Federal, state and local taxes which amount to several times the value of the product. Portugal has no excise tax on wine, which is generally cheaper there than beer. The Spanish pay less for their *ordinaire* than for their bottled drinking water! The general availability and wide use of wine in this country will be curtailed as long as it is looked upon as an alcoholic beverage instead of as a food. There's no more fitting occasion for a lover of wine to lift his voice in protest against such a miserable state of affairs than the beginning of a chapter like this.

The wisest piece of advice in Hilaire Belloc's little book called *Advice* is indubitably this: "Divide your buying of wine into two clear departments (1) Buying ordinary wine. (2) Buying special wine." Accordingly, we'll put off considering special wine 'til later. Like the quest for the perfect hamburger, the search for the best day-to-day drinking wine goes on indefinitely. More real connoisseurship probably goes into choosing everyday wine than all our enjoying of fine wines, because that's what we drink most of and besides, we are more limited by considerations of cost. When there's an occasion or excuse to buy a fine wine to drink for fun, the expense matters less to us. When looking for wine that won't violate our budget, however, we will be satisfied with *ordinaire* and pleased when we can find something better at the same price.

There are many imports that are cheap enough to drink every day, but there's no way to be sure of what you're getting. If you're prepared to experiment, there's no reason not to shop the 99-cent-to-$1.29 baskets featured in many a supermarket, drugstore, liquor shop and whatnot across the land. Spanish Riojas and Chilean Rieslings are almost unfailingly good buys. Other than that there are no general rules, since the import-export firms vary from state to state. More and more Spanish, Yugoslavian and even French wines are appearing with varietal names and vintage years; these are honestly labelled at least. Some of the 1959 Yugoslavian Cabernet we've bought at 99 cents the bottle has been really fine, but there's considerable variation from bottle to bottle and even more from type to type within any importer's line, so separating sheep from goats is purely a matter of trial and error. Buying French, German and Italian low-cost wines is riskiest of all. Without a reputable shipper's label, Liebfraumilch or Moselblümchen can be anything at all that was raised somewhere along the length of the Rhine or Moselle rivers. Even modestly priced, such wines are more often swindles than bargains. Then there are certain French firms which sell nothing at all in France but exist only to purvey inferior French wines to Americans. When it comes to cheaper wines, these countries export mainly bilge rejected by the natives when offered them at a fraction of the price for which it's sold to us. European *ordinaire,* on the whole, is far more ordinary than our own.

inexpensive imports

American wine-industry spokesmen and publicists speak of "standard wines" and "premium wines" to avoid the more subjective categories like *ordinaire,* good and so forth. Anything sold by the fifth in corked bottles is deemed "premium," whereas everything mass-produced and generally available by the jug is called "standard." Now as we've noted on a previous page, some so-called premium wine is great, and much of it is no better than it should be. By the same token, it won't do to call everything available by the jug "standard" wine. Some of it is quite ordinary, some not so ordinary, and

"premium" and "standard"

54

some quite good indeed. Now a generic wine can be made from any variety or combination of grapes, and most of our generic wines fall into the standard category. The most popular reds are thus Burgundy, Claret and Chianti; and Chablis, Sauterne and Rhine wines the most often-met-with whites. No one expects all Irish potatoes to come from Ireland or wants Wisconsin to stop producing Swiss cheese, but wine experts have long maintained that the only *true* Burgundy must come from the region of that name in France, and so on down the line. This purism—if such it be—is not really unfounded. Environment is infinitely more important than heredity in determining the character of the wine any given variety of grape will produce. Our generic wines have next to nothing in common with their namesakes. American-grown Sauterne is not so-called because of any imagined similarity to its namesake, but only because the public buys the name. Too often, there's no flavor difference whatever between the Chablis and Sauterne or Claret and Burgundy produced by a given winery: they just change the labels and maybe use a different-shaped bottle. Generic wines are invariably blends—and no two wineries have identical recipes for Chablis, say, or Burgundy, although virtually all market a wine of some sort under these names. As you might expect, therefore, the same generic names may describe wines that range from dreadful to just short of fine.

generic wines

The greatest part of our wine production, like everyone else's, consists of *ordinaire,* and almost all our *ordinaire* is sold under these generic names. The most notable exceptions are the ever bountiful Zinfandel and Barberone (Italian for "big Barbera"). Most of this production, moreover, is controlled by a very few corporations. It's been estimated that United Vintners (Italian Swiss Colony, Petri, et al.) and Gallo are between them responsible for at least 65 percent of California's wine. Franzia Brothers,

major mass producers

Guild and Carlo Rossi's Red Mountain are the other major firms competing in the arena of our cheapest wines. One is compelled to salute the technical expertise by which these companies produce what the Wine Institute dubs "sound standard wines." They are sound—we've never encountered a spoiled or nastified bottle—and they do constitute a standard against which any of the world's *ordinaire* might be measured. An unhealthy percentage of European *ordinaire* is downright undrinkable, and much of what is drunk would be very substandard indeed under California's regulations. Since the firms we've named rank as the largest wineries in the land, a book like this should not pass over their products without comment. On the other hand, a serious rating of their wines is out of the question, because no *ordinaire* is distinctive or complex enough to bear that much analysis. But for what it's worth, herewith the general impressions we've formed over a number of years.

red ordinaire

Franzia and Red Mountain are tied for the most all-round unpleasant generic wines, in our opinion. It was not always thus—by body count of dead soldiers we computed thirty-three gallons of Red Mountain Burgundy consumed in 1965. But these wines have changed for the worse with the times. Nowadays Petri puts out a "Crystal" brand Burgundy which ranks along with Italian Swiss Colony's red "Vino Primo" and its "Private Stock" line as the pick of the United Vintners' bunch. Gallo's "Hearty Burgundy" and "Paisano" seem to represent the best that firm can do with red wines. All these seem to have somewhat more body and aroma than their run-of-the-assembly-line relatives, and you don't seem to get tired of them quite as quickly as you do of the others. The Guild Wine Company is a cooperative best known for its "Vino da Tavola" and "Famiglia Cribari" brands. Though in the same price range as the other wines we've mentioned, they must be considered separately because they're made sweeter. Their greatest appeal is probably to people who've just started drinking wine, but if you've no objection to a little sweetness you'll find the red "Vino da Tavola" among California's more creditable *ordinaires.* "Famiglia Cribari" sports what is surely the most floridly soulful label of any California *ordinaire;* it is even sweeter and belongs in a category of its own.

For our taste, all these firms err on the side of sweetness when it comes to white wines, and we were never able to drink enough to offer any guidance. *Caveat emptor!* (An exception that comes to mind is the Sauterne which Guild puts out under the "Winemasters" label.) All these wineries except for Italian Swiss Colony get most of their grapes from California's Central Valley. Their "sound standard wines" make no claim to distinction and will usually do for any occasion when a wine's presence and wetness are more important than its taste.

white ordinaire

Now you know our prejudices concerning the most ubiquitous domestic brands. All of these are available in the half or full gallon. Chain stores in every locale will have comparably priced house brands also available in bulk. The thing to do is start with the cheapest and judge for yourself which of the bulk wines available to you are the best in their class. The list of contenders is almost endless if you happen to live in California, where much of the bulk wine is many cuts above *ordinaire* in quality. Our favorite red is Cambiaso Vintners Reserve Burgundy, which costs no more than Gallo by the gallon and surpasses all but the very best California Burgundies. Others swear by the reds or whites produced by D'Agostini, Emile, Louis Foppiano or Fortino Brothers. Nor should we omit mention of Parducci, one of the northernmost of our vineyards, producers of some of California's darkest rosé and crispest Chablis—fine wines for the price of *ordinaire.* But though deserving of great praise, these are local wineries whose products are

good wines available in bulk in California

doomed to be known only by hearsay outside the state. Such bounty, alas, cannot be shared across state lines.

The day-to-day consumption of good wine need cost no more (or little more) than *ordinaire* even outside California, if you're willing to hunt a little harder for it. You may have to search wine and liquor stores for the good bulk wines that some few wineries do market nationally. Prominent among them are Almadén, Christian Brothers, Inglenook, Louis M. Martini, C. Mondavi and Sons and Samuele Sebastiani. A knowledgeable merchant's advice can be helpful in choosing among the wines available from these companies, because you don't always get what you pay for. Their wines are sometimes no better—though usually drier—than those of their larger competitors. Unlike their competitors' products, moreover, they may vary noticeably from batch to batch. Mountain Red Claret is the most distinctive of Almadén's bulk line and the only one we think much above *ordinaire* grade. Christian Brothers Burgundy we've always found a very good wine and a bargain when it can be bought in bulk. Inglenook's half gallons are priced almost out of the economy class; all except the Grenache Rosé carry vintage dates. Except for the Zinfandel, the Inglenook reds generally seem less successful than the whites of theirs we've tried. Louis M. Martini's Mountain Red is very tart and very good indeed. His Mountain White we've found less dependable but still better than *ordinaire*. C. Mondavi & Sons market some of California's best bulk wines under the "CK" and "Mondavi Vintage" labels. The "CK" Barberone is one of the best buys in the country at under four dollars the gallon, and so is the "CK" Zinfandel which we happen to be drinking at the moment. "Mondavi Vintage" has never let us down. It costs about the same as Inglenook's bulk wine, but their whites in particular seem well worth the price. Samuele Sebastiani's Mountain Red and Mountain

good wines nationally available in bulk

White seem the least consistent in quality of any—"when they are good, they're very, very good"; when they're not, they're simply *ordinaire.*

We have not even tried to mention every one of the wines available in bulk in each of these best-selling brands so that you will feel encouraged to make discoveries and draw comparisons for yourself. The foregoing are simply our personal favorites among the most commonly available bulk wines, the wines we have found by experience to be consistently outstanding compared with all the others available in their price range. If you are buying *vin ordinaire,* or even something better than *ordinaire* but destined for the day-in-day-out dinner table, you have a right to expect certain things: first, that the wine be fruity, properly balanced and clean to the taste; second, that it be inexpensive; third, that it be what it claims to be. Try the different brands of generic wines—and Zinfandel and Barberone—until you hit on the red and the white that exactly suit your palate and your purse. Then lay in a supply commensurate with your storage space and your budget. Sooner or later, most wine drinkers get into the habit of buying in the largest quantities they can, not only to insure against running out of everyday wine but also to minimize trips to the wine store.

what to expect

If you make your purchases by the gallon, it's a good idea to rebottle your stock in fifths. In fact it's often a necessity. Once opened, a gallon of wine may easily spoil overnight, and even those that don't may begin to taste unpleasantly different after a few hours exposure to the air. This can happen whether the jug is recapped or not on account of the greater area of air-exposed surface inside the jug. Buying *ordinaire* for a party or picnic is another matter, of course, but when you're laying in a home supply to be consumed gradually, it's safest to rebottle your gallons or whatever in smaller quantities. We've found that it's least time consuming to rebottle two

rebottling

or three gallons at a time. Save (or scrounge) fifteen used bottles and corks. Boil the corks and rinse the bottles. Then sterilize the bottles by leaving them in your oven at 500 degrees Fahrenheit for half an hour. Allow them to cool completely, fill and cork. Voilà! You now have a steady supply of *ordinaire* for your table and a very present help in time of trouble. The storage space must be reasonably cool and dark with little change of temperature, and the bottles are happiest lying on their sides. A few suitably located cabinet shelves will serve admirably.

Young wines need a kind master and a good home in which to reach maturity. If you do have a basement or garage, or even closet space which is dark, dry and above all, cool and constant in temperature, get yourself some plywood and construct a few diamond-shaped bins. By dovetailing the bottlenecks, we've been able to get dozens and dozens of bottles into a single bin, two feet by two feet and eighteen-inches deep. A number of these enable you to retrieve the bottle you want without disturbing your whole cache. Thus prepared, you may buy your wines young and drink them old. Most fine reds are sold long before they are ready to drink, and the price of the small amount remaining sky rockets as the wine improves. Moreover, you can almost always get a 10-percent discount buying wines by the case.

So far we've been discussing table wines that can usually (though not always) be found in grocery stores and suchlike. In listing our favorite everyday wines, we've given as much guidance as we feel a book honestly can give. Few vintners are able to bottle, month in and month out, exactly the same blends under each of their type labels. There are several reasons for viewing with suspicion any volume offering extensive rankings and laborious comparisons of fine wines especially. Such a book would of necessity be more of an historical document than a consumer's guide by the time it was

storing wine
to age

61

distributed for sale because most of the wine considered would already have been sold. The very wines under discussion would moreover be changing constantly, some a little, some a lot, with age. And despite the "every year's a vintage year" publicity, California wines do vary from batch to batch like *book-learning* any others. Finally and most important, there can almost by definition be no objectivity in matters of taste. The same thing will taste different to the same person depending on whether he's fed or famished, tired or fresh, and so on. Experience and sensitivities vary from person to person also, producing different and equally valid judgments of the same characteristic in a wine of any complexity. A wine we pronounce "robust" may seem to have only medium body to you. The only way to come to know wine, and your own taste in wine, is to drink it.

This is not to say there's no need to seek wise guidance sometimes, and with wine at least the place to look for it is the right wine shop. It won't *the right* be the one with a display of wines in the window. If the merchant doesn't *wine shop* know that wines require protection from sunlight and heat, he isn't likely to know too much else about them. The importance of finding a good wine dealer can hardly be overestimated, for he (and not a writer) is the first and indispensable tutor in the buying of special wines. If you're lucky you may find several local shops where you can make purchases and get advice, but by all means choose dealers who drink wine themselves. They are always eager to pass on to you the love of wine they have acquired, and to share with you their many experiences, discoveries and surprises. If a dealer does not take evident pride in his profession and pleasure in discussing with you any wine, its virtues and limitations, before you buy it, he's not the man for you to patronize. Needless to add, no good wine dealer pushes a wine merely because it's expensive or uses snob appeal to try to make a sale.

A good dealer will tell you that the comparative value of different wines increases out of all proportion to prices. The cost of the bottle, shipping charges, taxes and so forth are the same for a fifth of *ordinaire* as for a fifth of something fine. A wine costing two dollars is usually much more than twice as good as a bottle selling for one, therefore, because all the extra goes entirely into the wine. This does not mean that you always get what you pay for, only that a wine that is too cheap is a wine that's too expensive. Fine wines cost dearly because there is never enough for everybody, the demand always exceeds the supply. Only considerable experience or sound advice can procure you the best bargain for your money every time you buy them.

buying special wines

The best way you can explore the world of fine wines confidently is to find a wine merchant whom you can trust completely to serve as advisor and guide. Besides, half the joy of wine comes from sharing your discoveries with an understanding and sympathetic friend and finding that you can hold your own in the many arguments that arise among wine lovers. It also helps to be able to read a wine label.

One could almost suspect the world's wine producers of conspiring to confuse the consumer with the sonorous words they use on their labels. In most cases there is literally no way the uninitiated can judge from its label how a bottle's contents will taste.

Both Federal and California law control what a wine label may and must not say; and confusing as they are, the California regulations on labelling furnish far more information as to flavor than any others in the world. Champagnes, for example, may be labelled "dry," *"sec,"* *"brut,"* *"nature,"* *"doux,"* or "extra dry." Each of these terms, used to designate degrees of sweetness, is carefully defined only in California's law. California's

California wine labels

regulations likewise distinguish among the phrases "produced and bottled," "made and bottled," "estate-bottled," and so forth. "Produced" means at least 75 percent of the wine in the bottle was crushed, fermented and matured by the vintner named. "Made" indicates the vintner was similarly responsible for less than 75 but a minimum of 10 percent of the wine thus labelled. "Bottled at the winery" is another phrase whose use is restricted but which means much the same as "produced." At the exclusive end of the spectrum is the legend "estate-bottled." This appears only when 100 percent of the grapes used were grown on that vineyard and every drop of the wine made in that winery. "Cellared," "perfected" or "prepared and bottled by" are also sometimes met with, and all mean only that the bottler put some finishing touches on the wine before calling it his. To satisfy the minimum Federal requirement a label must somewhere state "bottled by" with the bottler's name and place of business.

"produced" vs. "made"

The words "table wine" or "light wine" sometimes appear in the place of a statement of alcohol contents. Table wines, under California law, must be 10-to-14 percent alcohol, with a tolerance of 1-1/2 percent allowed. A statement of alcohol content is mandatory on all dessert wines, where the legal maximum is 21 percent alcohol and the tolerance only 1 percent.

Mandatory, likewise, is some statement of geographical origin. All the wine in bottles labelled "California" must be from grapes grown in the state. More specific designation, like "Livermore," "Sonoma," and so forth is allowed when at least 75 percent of the grapes used came from and were fermented in the place named. These requirements can be contrasted with those of other states like New York, which allows up to 25 percent of the grapes used in "New York" wines to be imported from elsewhere. And despite the admirable *"Appellation Contrôlée"* laws which apply to the more

place of origin

notable French wines, France is still the world's leading importer of wines in bulk for blending with its own production. As one expert has observed, the French are better at writing strict laws than they are at enforcing them. Indeed, most European *vins ordinaires* would probably be rejected as substandard under the minimum quality regulations in California. These have long been the strictest such standards in the world.

varietal labelling

California law is not nearly so strict when it comes to the actual names of wines, the most mysterious of all the words on the label. We have already noted that generic or type-named wines can be made from any and every grape. Most of the "premium" wines are given varietal names, the names of the grape variety from which they are made. Although most of our grapes are of European origin, the names of the different varieties are virtually unknown to the European public. Cabernet Sauvignon and Pinot Noir are familiar to millions of Americans, while Frenchmen who have been drinking the juice of these grapes all their lives will rarely have heard of them. In California as long as a minimum 51 percent of the wine comes from the grape named it is eligible for varietal labelling. True, the 49 percent must always play a silent-partner role so that the wine has the predominant characteristics of the variety designated, but the requirement is still ridiculously low. The better grapes are all very shy bearers, and the law is set up to enable wineries to market just about twice as much as they grow—if they feel like it. Not long ago Beaulieu proposed that the requirement for varietal labelling be raised to 75 percent, but only Louis M. Martini supported their proposal. There is certainly no need to make a fetish of one-variety winemaking for its own sake. Most varietals need blending somewhat to smooth and enhance the character of the main ingredient, but it's hard to believe the wine wouldn't be better if more of it really were what it claims to be. A varietal which carries a vintage date, however, is required to contain at least 75 percent of that variety, a fact worth remembering.

Now for a bit of Bacchic blasphemy on this matter of the vintage date! Vintage years are of very real importance in Europe. Years of bad weather, and thus of poorer wines, recur with such unpleasant frequency there that wine lovers are forced to learn which are the good years simply to avoid buying the bad ones. There's an average annual variation of something like 15 percent in the amount of sunlight suffusing California's vineyards, however, with the result that there simply are no spectacular differences between years in California wines. This does not mean that there are *no* differences, of course. The years 1948 and 1962 were considered less than satisfactory, and 1954, 1964 and 1968 extraordinary. The decreased quantity of wine which survived the disastrous late frost of 1970 should make that another excellent year. Wineries always differ in their success with a year's vintage anyway, and even in those years when most wine is fine, poor wine is also produced.

the vintage year

Vintage dates can be used on California wines only when all the grapes used in that wine were harvested and fermented in that year. Winemakers who do not vintage date their varietals often talk of the need for freshening older wine by blending some younger with it or say they want their wines to have the same flavor every year. What most of them probably really want is to avoid the problem of selling wines from reputedly poorer years and the requirement of using 75 percent of the designated variety in varietal wines. Every batch of wine will differ somewhat from every other, even in places where "every year's a vintage year," and blending does not produce unchanging aroma and flavor in wines from month to month, much less from year to year. Fortunately, more and more wineries are acknowledg-

vintage dating

ing this and using vintage dates. This not only makes it easier for us consumers to find other bottles of some particularly memorable nectar, but it also permits more intelligent comparisons between the same wines from different wineries. Most important, it tells the wine's birthday.

a matter of age

Any discussion of vintage dates calls for a digression on the related subject of aging. Most of the world's wines are consumed before they are even a year old for the very good reason that they would get no better if they were stored longer. Unfortunately, very few of the California wines which do profit from bottle aging are allowed time to mature. Beginning in 1970, thankfully, the government stopped taxing vintners and merchants on their entire warehouse inventory every year, which had made the proper aging of certain wines on their premises prohibitively costly. Not all fine wines require aging, of course. Each has its own time for reaching maturity, staying at its peak, and then beginning to fade. Whites, on the whole, will have attained their optimum fragrance and flavor within a year or so of vintage, though some people prefer them at three or four years. Rosés are often best at about six months. Red wine generally needs more time to reach its best, but this varies. Some Cabernet Sauvignon may well be undrinkable until it has passed the five-year mark and may continue to improve for decades thereafter, while most Beaujolais or Red Pinot is usually long past its prime at the end of a decade. Zinfandel may be drunk as young or as old as you like. "Old wine, like old friends, the best," is thus a blanket inaccuracy, even if some poet did say it. Age is *not* the noblest of all vinous virtues; except in the case of certain fine and long-lived reds, age is deceptive as an indication of quality. If you want to know how old a wine without a vintage date is, try looking at the bottom of the bottle. Most manufacturers of American wine bottles blow into the bases of their bottles a record of the year in which they were made, usually two digits next to the hallmark ('68, '69, '70). Figuring that the better wineries keep their reds in the wood for at least two years before bottling, the whites one year, and the rosés under a year, you can determine the age of the wine fairly accurately.

To return now to our labels. You frequently find on them strange numbers or words like "private stock," "private reserve" or "limited bottling." None of these terms is regulated by law; they can indicate higher quality wines, or they can be entirely without meaning and intended only to impress. Cask, *cuvée* and bin numbers are the most mystifying because no explanation of their deeper meanings is ever found on the labels that carry them. They just conceivably may help you identify wine from some particular batch that you liked so that you can get more of the same. Anyway, they look impressive. Your only guide as to whether or not to ignore all such notations as these must be the reputation of the individual wineries involved and, of course, the good advice of your wine dealer. Our glossary should be useful in unravelling the intricacies of foreign wine labels, but you must also look to the good offices of your wine merchant for aid. If he's worthy of your trust, you may learn a great deal from him about the judicious selection of wine. Someone you may *not* trust nine times out of ten is the *sommelier,* wine steward or wine waiter from whom you order your wine in a restaurant. Rest assured the restaurant will make a very handsome profit on whatever wine you order there; most charge at least 100 percent more than a liquor store would for the same bottle. The less likely its clientele is to be familiar with a given wine, the more likely the restaurant is to charge even more for it. In too many places part of the sommelier's job is simply to sell its highest-priced vintages. On the other hand, the least expensive wines are usually the ones with the highest markups. The best buys on the wine list

the indecipherable

the sommelier

69

generally lie somewhere between these extremes. Unless you know the restaurant, trusting to the selection of a waiter may procure you no more than an expensive name and not necessarily an appropriate wine.

The conditions in which wine is kept in restaurants and the handling it receives are with few exceptions far from ideal. Unless you can afford (at their prices) to risk a disappointing bottle, it's a good idea to order the finest wines only when you know all about the restaurant and have good reason to trust it. The best wines, such as better restaurants pride themselves on stocking, cannot be whisked to your table in a state ready for immediate consumption. After all, it has been imprisioned in its bottle perhaps ten years awaiting your summons, and deserves a chance to take the air, to stretch and expand, before it can possibly be expected to put on its best performance. It's criminal not to allow a very fine or great wine half an hour, say, between the time it's uncorked and the time you drink it. In fact, all red wines should profit from being allowed such a breathing space so that the bouquet can really blossom and show off. You'll have to arrange this with the waiter since it is unfortunately not common practice in this country.

ordering wine in restaurants

It's too much to ask of any wine that it go well with any wide gastronomic variety. If there's no unanimity about the food your party wants, neither can there by any about the wine. If you are all determined to drink the same wine together, there's always Champagne or rosé. These may represent the easiest choice, but in our opinion they are rather a poor compromise. There's always that certain wine we think would set off some dish to perfection, and it seems a pity to do without it. The only solution then is to order more than one kind of wine, either a one-tenth bottle for each person or a whole bottle of both red and white. White wines need no time to breathe, but it's a good idea to have them arrive at the table early

ordering more than one

also. If the wine has been in a bin somewhere, it will need some little while in an ice bucket to cool. If it's just come from a refrigerator, it may well be too cold and need time to warm.

In due course the wine steward returns with your selection(s) and goes into his act with the corkscrew, first showing you the label so you know you are getting what you ordered. If he doesn't offer you the cork, ask to see it. Look at it. If the bottom is wine soaked then the wine has been stored properly on its side. Smell it. If it smells like cork—and not like wine—the wine is almost surely corky. If the sommelier is especially pretentious, you may want to bite the bloody cork just to watch his reaction. Then he will pour a half inch into your glass and await your judgment. The first thing to look out for is corkiness, an uncommon but unmistakeable disorder, a fierce *when to send* mustiness that assaults nose and palate immediately. Many a good bottle has *wine back* other funny smells immediately upon opening, so if you're not pleased with your first sniff, swirl the wine for a while and see if the odor goes away. Whites may be tainted with sulphur, and reds sometimes have something mildewy about them. If these smells persist and are confirmed by the taste, you've got a bad bottle and should send it back. Any restaurant will take back bottles so afflicted. If it's been stored too long in a place too hot for it, the wine will taste dead and despondent and should also be sent back.

Sending back wine which has no gross defects but simply is not up to expectations depends, we suppose, on how sure you are of what that wine ought to be. Few restaurants will risk alienating business by starting an argument over the matter if you look as though no discussion is going to change your mind. Remember that you're not bound to accept what's offered you, in any case, and it's a shame to accompany a really good meal with a less-than-satisfactory wine.

WINE SERVING
What goes with what?

Do what thou wilt shall be the whole of the Law

—Aleister Crowley

erving wine requires nothing more than a corkscrew and some glassware. Both deserve some comment. The ideal corkscrew exists only in heaven. The wide variety of corkscrews existing on earth all have something wrong with them. Many are exasperating and some are dangerous. With most you must put the bottle between your knees, holding it with the left hand and fighting the often reluctant cork with your right. This method can rupture the puller and, if he has a weak heart, kill him stone dead. This perilous waste of effort often accomplishes nothing anyway. A better sort of corkscrew does all the work mechanically, either by means of levers or else with a fancy reverse-action screw on top which lifts the cork out as if it were pulled by a giant. These are generally much more satisfactory than the first kind, but they also have their deficiencies. The lever-principle ones lead rather sooner than later to scraped knuckles. The reverse-action, lift-out types usually either have worms with cutting edges or worms that are not long enough for all corks. Thus even when you're able to get the worm in, you run the risk of tearing the center out of an old cork with all that added mechanical power.

earthly corkscrews

Our favored implement at the moment of writing is an ingenious item of Danish design which is not, in fact, a corkscrew at all. It consists of a wooden handle with two flat and tapering metal fangs attached and requires a very patient operator in order to work. You insert the flat metal pieces on either side of the cork and gradually work them down between it and the neck of the bottle. By alternating pressure from side to side very cautiously, you finally get the metal pieces past the cork, then twisting this way and that you draw it out easy as pie. Our research has failed to turn up the

manufacturer's name, but the one we own has the word "Gourmet" inscribed on the wooden handle. Patiently applied, it works very well for us most of the time. It doesn't work at all when the bottle neck slopes away from the cork a few deceptive fractions of an inch inside the lip of the bottle. We've discovered that bottles thus fiendishly engineered come mainly from Germany and Argentina.

the heavenly corkscrew

From the foregoing it should be obvious that we may as well resign ourselves to the utter depravity of inanimate objects. Still, it is helpful to envision the characteristics of the heavenly corkscrew while we are shopping for yet another one to try out. It has, to begin with, a worm long enough to transfix even the longest cork. The point is not dead center, but rather exactly in line with its spirals. These are without cutting edges, and there's an open space down the center. And lastly, we are confident the good God has contrived a mechanism which eliminates tugging and muttered curses. But until this device is bequeathed us mortals, we can only go on looking for the corkscrew that combines most of these attributes in itself.

glassware

If the simple matter of the best corkscrew is complicated, the complicated question of the "right" glassware is simple. Manufacturers, advertisers and salesmen of glassware would all have us believe that Burgundy and Claret, Rhine and Moselle, are each properly served only in its own distinctively shaped glass. They convinced our grandmothers this was the case, and bars and restaurants reinforce these old-fashioned affectations today. There is even a "proper" glass for serving rosé d'Anjou! All this has made for good business ever since Victorian days, but it's played hell with good sense. A squadron of wineglasses beside every place setting may be a pretty sight, but they make no difference to the taste of the wine that's served in them and this is what really counts. Only people hopelessly brainwashed by crystal salesmen and Madison Avenue can still pretend there are such creatures as "proper" glasses for different wines. ("And this is the Chianti glass in our new Corinthian candle pattern, Madam.") The truth of the matter is a glass that's good for any wine is a good glass for every wine.

Good wineglasses show off the wine; therefore they are not tinted or ornamented in any way that distorts the wine's color. A good wineglass is large enough to hold half a pint, or almost. This way when half full it holds a reasonable amount and still leaves plenty of room at the top for the bouquet to collect. So that you can get bouquet and taste all at once, there should be room for your nose inside the rim when you tip your glass to drink from it. And so that you can swirl the wine to your heart's content and not lose any of its perfumes, a good wineglass has to be tulip shaped. The ideal wineglass, in short, is any big, clear, tulip-shaped piece of stemware that's not too costly to replace nor so fragile as to require replacement often.

the ideal glass

But what of Champagne, Sherry and brandy glasses you ask? A few concessions, but no quarter. Unless you're a glassware hobbyist, that Victorian trinket, the Sherry glass, should hold no more charm for you than it will Sherry. The largest, filled brimfull won't hold a decent-sized drink. They are easily spilled. In Spain, Sherry's native land, it is always served in glasses like our all-purpose, tulip-shaped stemware.

It's no compliment to Helen of Troy that some wag supposed our latter-day Champagne glasses were modelled on her breasts. Actually, of course, these glasses date from the same period that gave us the tuxedo and a host of similar social "refinements." Sparkling wines have scent like any other, but both scent and effervescence are only wasted in Champagne glasses. Try to smell the bouquet and you just get bubbles in your nose; you'd be better off drinking your Champagne out of slippers. The oldest

Champagne glasses

Champagne glasses we've ever seen were of pressed glass and made in Waterford, Ireland, around 1780. They were frosted—champagne makers had not yet discovered how to eliminate the sediment—and shaped like regular wineglasses more or less but had hollow stems. Hollow-stemmed glasses show off the effervescence to advantage and retain it longer, but special glasses are not really necessary for Champagne—the all-purpose glassware we've described serves admirably. Just by all means avoid that saucer-on-a-stem called a Champagne glass.

The all-purpose glass is also perfectly adequate for brandy, though you may find the traditional brandy-snifter shape with its shorter stem easier to handle. The idea is to stimulate the volatile fumes by warming the brandy with the palm of your hand; the thinner the glass is, therefore, the headier your brandy's bouquet.

If you do happen to own a cabinet full of glassware, you'll want to use your largest for Burgundies, your slightly smaller, narrower glasses for white and/or Bordeaux-type red wines, and the ones with the longest stems for the various Alsatian and Rhine-type wines. On the other hand, if you do not happen to own such a variety of glasses, there's really no necessity for acquiring them. Of course it is convenient to have enough glasses of some sort to serve two or more wines at a meal without having to wash up between courses.

sediment A corkscrew and glasses of some sort are all the special equipment you need to enjoy wine. But there are a few things to consider before you raise the first glass to your lips. An old red wine may have thrown a sediment during its years in the bottle. This is only natural, and in most cases the taste of the wine would be unaffected even if you drank all the dregs off. Being frankly lazy, we prefer just to handle such bottles gently and pour carefully and manage to avoid getting much sediment in any but the last glass or two.

If you're unhappy at the thought of drinking sediment or want your wine to be perfectly brilliant in the glass, decanting is the only answer. Take care not to stir up the sediment while handling and opening the bottle; then gently pour the wine from its original bottle into a decanter in front of a white surface or a light. When the light reveals tiny specks swimming past, it's time to stop pouring. Decanting is something you'll rarely need to bother with, but whenever possible you will want to open your red wines an hour or more before drinking them. Some people do this with white wines too. It certainly doesn't hurt them, but it's never seemed to improve white nearly as much as red wine. This chance to take the air makes the wine much livelier and more fragrant. Try it sometime with two bottles of the same wine, opening one an hour beforehand and the other immediately before drinking. You'll be amazed at the difference and begin to think, as we do, that you're not really getting the full pleasure when the wine you drink hasn't been allowed time to breathe.

giving
wine breathing space

There's also the question of Fahrenheit and centigrade to consider before you get around to drinking your wine. Rosés and whites, it's generally agreed, are better chilled and reds somewhat below normal room temperature. But to some people chilled means icy and to others barely cool. You'll find if wine is very cold it doesn't have much smell to it (which explains all those labels instructing "serve very well chilled"). Some people make much of the "ideal" temperature for this white or that—too much, actually, for the wine is mouth temperature soon after it passes our lips. It's up to you— there's no such thing as a right temperature. Lots of people also refrigerate their Sherry and Port. Adjusting wine's temperature and letting it breathe are not mandatory, but wine—as the wise old ancients knew—is in reality a god

temperature

and will pay you back with added pleasure for every premeditated courtesy you show it.

A liter of wine contains an eighth of a man's nourishment and nine-tenths of his good humor, as some anonymous authority has noted truthfully. Nobody ever heard of a man enjoying a good wine and going out to assassinate another. And it's demonstrably nourishing. Wine's greatest contribution to the betterment of mind and body, however, comes from the power it possesses to complement the finest food and compensate for the poorest. Pray take note, however; there are some few foods and condiments *known no-no's* with which any wine tastes terrible and which will taste terrible with wine. Our unpleasant experiences over a number of years have produced this rather Rabelaisian list: anchovies, candied yams, citrus fruits, all pickles, smoked herring, bananas, Boston baked beans, curries, chocolates, horseradish, molasses, and Worcestershire, mint and Tabasco sauces. Also mustard, and especially vinegar. Vinegar is probably wine's worst enemy. (M. de Caso's culinary genius, thankfully, has devised a final solution to the salad problem: hearts of lettuce with salt and pepper, olive oil and dry-wine dressing. Wines will go with this and this goes with wines!) There are, no doubt, other dishes and sauces which spoil wine as completely as all of the above, but these are the known offenders to date. Beware!

As for what goes with what, the title of this chapter, you're really on *out-of-fashion* your own. "Red wine with red meats, white with white, anything with *tastes* rosé!" is not inscribed somewhere on a tablet of stone. Such rules are made to be broken, if not ignored. Brillat-Savarin, that greatest of French gourmandisers and author of *The Physiology of Taste,* has nothing whatever to say about which wines and foods make the best companions. His contemporary, Napoleon, loved his savory, full-bodied Chambertin Burgundy with practically everything he ate. Even the epicures of the late nineteenth century would flabbergast a present-day wine steward with their ideas of the right wine to accompany the various courses of a formal dinner. The idea of ending a meal with shrimp canapés and a very sweet Sherry might induce convulsions today, but it was once done. The wine lover is an ultraconservative creature, and it takes a lot to induce him to give up his old habits for something new, however good it may be. But however slowly, habits and taste do change, and the best taste teaches us we need not indenture ourselves to the prejudices prevailing in our own times. We're not only entitled to our own eccentricities, we should encourage others in theirs.

aperitifs

The most that can be said for the combinations of wine and food that follow is that we like them. There are, of course, any number of wines people drink as aperitifs before the food appears. This seems to us the best of all the many uses to which dry Champagne can be put. Sweet drinks often tend to depress rather than stimulate the appetite, but this depends upon the individual and there's no need to avoid sweet aperitifs. If you haven't already, you should consider the bitter ones. We personally would choose a Campari on ice over any Sherry or Vermouth, sweet or dry. Sherry does go wonderfully well with clear soups—goes well in them too, and Marsala perhaps even better. A preliminary glass of whatever wine you're having with the meal makes an excellent appetizer-drink too, especially when you're having something white and chilled.

alliances with reds

Except for certain soufflés, egg dishes are treacherous. Many don't get along well with wine—fine wine at least. Young Zinfandel or Chianti have no nuances to lose and will stand up to an omelette very nicely. For the same reason, Chianti or Barbera are the obvious choices to go with spicy pastas like lasagna and spaghetti. Choice cuts of red-blooded meat which is not so highly seasoned as to overpower the finesse of a fine wine will admirably accompany the finest you can put beside it. There are many very good, unpretentious wines like Chateauneuf-du-Pape which combine well with good, unpretentious items like sausage or liver and bacon. Boeuf Bourguignon provides an excellent excuse for a bottle of the best French Burgundy you can find. Some like lighter wines with lamb —Beaujolais or Red Pinot—but Cabernet Sauvignon may have been created chiefly in order *lamb* to accompany this divinest of meats. Game always calls for red wines, supposedly, but we found Charles Krug Chenin Blanc and sweeter Rhine types set off the last venison we had as admirably as any red could. A regrettable lack of venison has held up further research. Southern specialties like fried rabbit or baked bob white would surely be affronted by white wines though. Cornish game hen, turkey and chicken are neutral dishes, so to *poultry* speak, that can be adapted to go with practically any wine. When prepared with a wine sauce, the chicken is ordinarily best served with that same wine. Roast turkey perhaps forms the best of all possible backgrounds for a great wine—be the wine white or red.

When you come to the meats which are without red blood and strong *white meats* savor, principally pork and veal, it's best to avoid the more forceful red wines. Indeed, we tend to avoid reds altogether with such fare in favor of full-bodied whites which have some suggestion of sweetness: certain Sauvignons Blancs and Rieslings are perfect. A light red or rosé may please you more. There's never been a "traditional" wine to go with ham, apparently. A large minority would match it with a Claret perhaps, but a dry rosé would be the choice of most people.

The fruit of the sea in all its multitudinous forms is almost always allied with white wines. We say almost, for among other experiments we *fish* have tried hot baked salmon with twelve-year-old Margaux and found the combination really excellent. (Salmon usually takes to whites of great character—Meursault, excellent Pinot Chardonnays and such.) We also enjoy good red wine with bouillabaisse the same way people in New Orleans do. But these are about the only cases that come to mind where red wines really enhance fishy flavors. We generally find the more acidic white wines which tend to offset any sharp fishiness go best with fish dishes. Oysters, crab meat, shrimp and especially lobster taste splendid indeed with such light, tart wines as Pinot Blanc, Chablis, dry Graves, Pouilly-Fuissé, et cetera, depending on what's available and what you feel like drinking, generally the drier the better. Fish with cream sauces or any strongly flavored fish will take to richer, heavier whites—dry Semillon, Pinot Chardonnay, Traminer and company—than will flaky, delicate sole, flounder, whitefish and such, when cooked in butter or simply broiled.

With cheeses, red wines are often better than whites, especially when the cheese is strong enough to walk away under its own power. Some of these can smother any wine except maybe heavy old Port. The cream or cottage cheese that often goes along with a soup or chicken salad luncheon seems made for the rosé appropriate to such occasions. Fruits (other than citrus varieties, remember) are also good with white or red, sweet or dry

desserts wines. Sweet desserts are often matched with sweet dessert wines, but different sweetnesses often seem to us to battle one another. A glass of Barsac, Muscat de Frontignan or a really luscious Château d'Yquem (three or four glasses!) are by themselves enough to put a perfect finish on a meal.

There are a few other discoveries we've made. Chinese food, for example, can be even more exotic with, say, Green Hungarian, Chenin Blanc or any such white, semi-sweet "little" wine. Also: if you're eating Mexican

food, drink beer! That's it to date: a rapid and disorderly review of some of our favorite alliances between foods and wines. There are further suggestions listed separately with each wine in the back of the book, to be discarded or disbelieved at will. The idea of "classic harmonies" is not an outright hoax, but the idea is too strait-laced to allow much experimentation and thus can misguide rather than help us discover our individual tastes. The vast majority of the world's wine drinkers, let us not forget, consume the one wine they produce locally with everything they eat, all their lives. They'd laugh at anybody who told them they were wrong.

"classic harmonies"

A gracious little habit to observe in serving wine is to pour an inch or so (less than a full serving) into your own glass first. "Pouring the cork," as it's called, insures that any bits of cork in the wine go into the glass of the host. After serving everybody else you can come back to your own glass and give yourself a full serving. This is customary because it's considerate, not because it looks nice. This brings us to some *sec* and *demi-sec* remarks on matters of so-called ritual. Even today the neo-Emily Postites are engaged in rear-guard action to enforce the most ostentatious ceremonial in serving wine. They deplore the appearance of cocktails before, or cigarettes with wine. They insist the bottle can be brought to the table only if ensconced in a wine cradle or wrapped in a napkin. They have elaborate theories about the order in which guests should be served and the correct wines for each course of a meal.

pomp and circumstances

Working our way backward through this list, we've already seen that the "correct" wines are the ones we enjoy. Unless you're sufficiently taste blind to serve Champagne with candy, you're in no danger of serving an "incorrect" one. Good manners would dictate that one's guests be served as unobtrusively as possible, so any order that's most convenient would be the one that's most correct. Some people find wire or wicker cradles handy for holding a bottle they intend to decant in one position while they open it; apart from this, the cradle has no function at all. A napkin may prevent a bottle that is wet from chilling in an ice bucket from dripping, but there's no real necessity for using one even then, and it would be purest affectation any other time. Rather than take the edge off your sensitivity, you may want to forego the martini and tobacco when you're expecting to drink a wine such as you are not likely to taste again for six months or a year. If you're drinking a great wine, something you expect to waft you away with unearthly delight, it would be downright foolish and disrespectful to drink cocktails before the wine appeared or to smoke while it is before you. But then it all depends on you. God knows there's plenty of smoking at the professional winemen's great gourmet banquets in Europe. What the little old ladies of both sexes forget when they formulate rules for serving wine is that wine is primarily for enjoyment, and not for show.

If you're planning to serve different wines with the several courses of a meal, however, you'll find that you enjoy each of the wines more if you figure out beforehand the best order in which to serve them. If menus and memoirs are to be believed, our ancestors could appreciate a succession of five or six fine wines at a sitting. They were made of sterner stuff. The age of apartment-house living has witnessed a decline in formal dining. We remember no American dinner where more than four wines were served with the food, and even that seems a bit excessive. In our view, the best wine at a meal is best served last. Likewise, it seems advisable to work up to the high point of the meal: you appreciate a great wine all the more if it's the only one on the menu. White wines are almost always more charming and better tasting when drunk before red wines. (If it's a sweet white wine it belongs at

wines in succession

the end of the meal with dessert, or can be served *for* dessert.) Fortified wines like Sherry or sparkling wines like Champagne may precede or follow anything, but they generally play havoc with your palate when served *between* still table wines.

Serving more than one red or white with a meal provides an opportunity to experiment with all sorts of comparisons and contrasts. You might have different Burgundies of the same vintage, or different vintages of the same Burgundy. You can contrast a fine California Cabernet Sauvignon with a fine French Claret. You may also enjoy very dissimilar wines at the same meal, but in this case it's especially wise for the wines to run in an ascending scale: "little" wines before the "big" ones, and young ones before the old ones, generally speaking. All this comparing is the more interesting when you have friends at hand to disagree with you. Serving more than one wine from time to time will remind you that the differences in vintages or between two wines of the same family are far from imaginary. Comparing one wine with the taste of another is obviously more difficult in memory than when they are served one after the other.

quantity   To conclude, some words on quantity may be in order. The capacity for wine varies enormously from person to person of course. As an overall average, however, a fifth-sized bottle will serve three and often four people of moderate thirst throughout a typical meal. Naturally, the richer and more plentiful the food, the more wine you will want and the more you can consume without any noticeable effect. An outright feast may enable all hands to down well over two bottles of wine apiece and risk no loss of composure. But the food had better be very rich indeed and the meal very leisurely should you want to test this statement. One or two glasses of white wine are usually enough to wash down a fish course when you plan to have

meat with a red wine afterwards. A half bottle is plenty for two people, or a whole bottle for three or four in such cases. A bottle of Sherry provides twelve servings of two ounces each, or enough for six people if everyone wants a second glass. If you're having a dry Champagne before dinner, or a sweet Champagne with dessert (heavenly!) you can figure on six glasses to the bottle, with a little more than four ounces to the glass. For receptions and similar functions, you're pretty safe allowing one bottle of champagne for every two or three persons.

Finally, don't drink wine if you mean to drug yourself with alcohol. In the first place, you can't really appreciate what you're drinking once you are drunk. In the second place, as Kipling put it

It's no time for mirth and laughter

That cold grey dawn of the morning after.

hangover

Overindulgence in wine produces a hangover of memorable and surpassing intensity. The best thing to do about a hangover is to avoid it. This is easily accomplished if at the first signs of inebriation you consume copious droughts of water, which God in His infinite mercy has obviously intended as the antidote to drunkenness. But there are certain sins for which the quality of mercy simply will not be strained, and God offers no antidote for the hangover. The Italians do. It contains every herb from aloes to zedoaria and is the one aperitif you will want to consume in strictest moderation since it can be a remarkably effective laxative if overdone. It's called Fernet-Branca and most people find it vile beyond belief. We admit it's the furthest-out flavor in Christendom, but it helps.

WINEMAKING
What do they do to it?

Wine is a living thing. It is made, not only of grapes and yeasts, but of skill and patience. When drinking it remember that to the making of that wine has gone, not only the labor and care of years, but the experience of centuries.

Allan Sichel

he flavor of wine starts on the vine. "Viticulture," Idwal Jones has observed, "is a profound and ancient art. The simplest of farmers, if it is their calling, may triumph in it; the ablest of scientists may be baffled by it." Raising grapes is year-round work. As soon as one year's vintage is over, the next year's cultivation begins. A grapevine will live fifty or sixty years if allowed its natural span (and many have lasted much longer), but for optimum yield most vineyards in this country replace their

viticulture vines every thirty-five years or so. New rootstock is set out and in the fall of its first growing season comes time to graft onto it the variety carefully selected for that particular piece of ground. Stakes are driven into place to support each vine; some of the nobler grapes will be trained along wires between the stakes. There is no significant yield for the first four or five years. Then before springtime the vineyard must be pruned.

Man learned grafting and pruning at some midpoint between the time of Noah and Virgil whose Latin verses give directions as precise as only a farmhand's could be, and the work is done by hand today the same as always. "Her vine," the Duke of Burgundy in Shakespeare's *Henry V* laments in time of war, "the merry cheerer of the heart, unprunèd, dies." While it may not die "unprunèd," it certainly loses its vigor and lessens its yield. Skillful pruning determines the arrangement of the next season's fruit on the vine. Finally, the vineyard must be weeded before spring brings the tender new growth and the time of waiting.

Will there be frost, rain, drought, fog? Anxiety over the weather welds wine men to their vineyards. A five-minute hailstorm can wipe out a year's growth. At intervals the vines must be sprayed to ward off blight:

pesticide to prevent leafhoppers, sulphur dust to guard against Oidium fungus. As soon as the leaves are old enough for the rabbits to lose interest in them, they become attractive to the deer. The ripening grapes must be shared with the bees and the birds. Whether it's a good year depends upon the amount of sunshine, but all the influences that affect the quality of the wine cannot be read on the temperature chart. There are other, more mysterious factors too subtle to be recorded. A favorable drift of air, or moonlight, or some inexplicable stir among the bacteria in the soil or in the bloom or fuzz of the grape all have their effect. Tests for sugar and acid are made more and more frequently until finally the vineyard owner decrees it time the harvest begin. The work, gruelling and sweaty, proceeds swiftly.

Scientists will probably never be able to define wine adequately in purest scientific terms. Chemical and other analyses have revealed to date over one hundred and fifty constituent elements in wine and the list, no doubt, will get longer. Despite this accumulation of research, laboratory experiments aimed at producing synthetic wine have never succeeded. It remains the product of grapes and yeast, two forms of plant life which mysteriously bring forth a third living substance—wine. Just as the egg must be fertilized, the grape juice or must requires for its transformation the attack of bacteria. For some reason, so long as the grapes remain on the vine this cannot occur. From the very moment when a bunch of grapes is picked, however, or sometimes even a little bruised, the bacteria begin their work of metamorphosis and the birth of the wine has begun. The winemaker does not really make the wine, therefore, he merely helps nature accomplish her work perfectly. He is thus a kind of pediatrician: he must be professionally competent but also a little inspired and very patient, for the process can last a number of weeks. He adds yeasts to insure victory over the bad ferments which would turn the developing wine into vinegar. He must keep the fermentation from stopping or getting "stuck" before it has finished. He must guard against a possibly fatal fever. But mainly he can only watch and wait until it is time for him to fill out the official forms, the birth certificate of the new vintage. Virtually all the wines of the Northern hemisphere are born Libra or Scorpio.

The grapes are brought from the fields directly to the crusher which removes the stems. The grape skins, pulp and must go directly into the vats or huge glass-lined tanks. In the case of white wines, the must is first separated from the skins. All grapes have white juice, and either black or white grapes may be used for white wines. The color of wine comes from the inside of the grape skin. Since these pigments are soluble in alcohol, the skins *black grapes* of white wine grapes must be separated from the must before fermentation *white grapes* begins. Rosés are left to ferment on the skins for a short time. Reds are left longer, until the sugar content of the must is between 2 and 8 percent. Then the wine-to-be is pumped into other casks or tanks to complete fermentation. The winemaker regularly takes the temperature of the bubbling and hissing liquid and checks its sugar content. White wines are generally fermented in *closed* containers at temperatures between 50 to 60 degrees Fahrenheit; while reds, in *open* containers while on the skins, ferment at temperatures up to 85 degrees. Once the developing wine has been separated from its "pomace" (pulp, skins, et cetera), it should complete its fermentation without exceeding 70 degrees. If the heat in the vats is not controlled, it may kill off the yeasts and put a premature end to their industrious activity.

Up until the Second World War the best reds might be left on the skins for two weeks or more. The large amount of tannin imparted by the grape seeds over such a period rendered the new wine harsh, often to the

point of undrinkability, until it had been allowed to age in the bottle for a number of years. Nowadays, most winemakers both in California and abroad leave their reds on the skins for an average of four to six days. The wine that results has less tannin and consequently matures earlier. Fifteen years ago, for instance, Beaulieu aged their Georges de Latour Reserve Cabernet Sauvignon for eight years before it was marketed, today it is put up for sale after only four years: a difference of four years in the bottle!

When fermentation is finished, the wine receives its first "racking." It is drawn off the lees (sediment in the fermenting vat) into cooperage for aging. White-oak barrels and casks holding from fifty to a thousand gallons allow just enough air to filter through the pores for the wine to breathe a

in the wood little, but not too much. The size and sort of cooperage depends on the wine. Oak or redwood tanks with a capacity of several thousand gallons may be used. Evaporation also occurs while the wine is in the wood, and loss on the order of 8 to 10 percent (including loss from the lees) is not unusual for the first year. Every few weeks therefore each barrel must be "topped up to the bung," that is filled to the barrel hole, to prevent the harm too much air contact would cause. This is called "ullage."

Now the wine has been delivered, but no one can tell what future awaits the newborn, although the winemaker can readily see whether it is plump or thin, healthy or sickly. But if it is born into the nobility, he must await the springtime, when the wine is six months of age, more or less, before he can with some accuracy judge what qualities are latent within it and how the youngster should be reared. The growth and development of a new wine is determined by a series of extremely complex actions and interactions about which almost nothing is known. Like every other form of life, wine needs to breathe, and oxidation is the chief influence in its development. But if it is to develop properly, wine should have less and less oxygen the older it gets. Whites and rosés require less than reds, generally speaking, and some reds need much more than others. How a wine is treated and stored thus depends upon its nature and its age.

American winemakers generally choose to rack their wines less and filter them more often than their European counterparts. Racking is like taking the wine out for a little walk in the fresh air; it not only clarifies but also promotes aging by speeding up oxidation. The lees that are left behind consist mainly of microscopic particles of soil, dead microbes, bits of cream of tartar, flecks of grape skin and suchlike dreck. The ever-attentive wine-master, tasting and analyzing, must also decide when the wine is ready for "fining." On every step in winegrowing and winemaking there are at least two opposing schools of thought, but fining methods defy enumeration. The idea is a sort of reverse filtering whereby the filter passes through the wine instead of vice versa. Gelatin and casein are probably the fining agents most often employed by California wineries, but there are many who swear by more traditional materials like egg white, isinglass, skim milk or beef blood. Whatever is used is spread in a thin veil over the wine and given a number of days or weeks to settle out, collecting on its way to the bottom any infinitesmal particles that may be suspended in the wine. After fining comes the real filtration(s) and the filters employed are often fine enough to trap microbes. If the wine is blended, it is allowed a "marrying" period to see whether it requires additional treatment.

racking fining

At last the winemaster judges his vintage properly clarified and sufficiently aged for bottling. The wine has come of age. It will not stop developing in its new glass home, but the process will be slower since it must henceforth breathe through a cork. As we have noted elsewhere, the size of

"bottle sickness"

97

the bottle will naturally determine the rate at which bottle aging occurs. The wine is then binned for at least six months until its inevitable "bottle sickness" passes and it has acclimatized itself to its enclosure.

Most wines, let us remember, receive no such upbringing as we have described, and moreover do not deserve it. *Ordinaire* comprises perhaps nine-tenths of the total annual wine production. It is ready to drink within months, if not days, of fermentation. Much of this produce has been stabilized to death by the time it is put on the market and is equally impervious to boiling or freezing. Otherwise of course it would be unequal to the tribulations of shipment and mass merchandising it must endure after it leaves the winery. The American mania for perfect clarity in our beverages induces even our premium-wine producers to overtreat even their best wines. Most of the shiny equipment you will find in modern wineries is not used for making wine but for filtering and stabilizing it so that it will stay perfectly brilliant. Some of the fresh fruity grape aromas and flavors are inevitably sacrificed to avoid any sort of sediment which might offend the eye of the mighty American consumer.

mass production

How the desired degree of clarity and stabilization is achieved in our mass-produced *ordinaire* we shall leave to your imagination. The technology of mass-producing wine is very different anyway: pasteurization, heat treatment to extract the red color from grapeskins before rather than during fermentation, and similar shortcuts are common practice. Let us, therefore, leave the mysterious methods of these manufacturers veiled in a decent obscurity. By way of reassurance, we hasten to add that their operations have absolutely nothing in common with those of which Addison (or was it Steele?) so quoteably complained over two hundred years ago:

"There is in this city a certain fraternity of chemical operators, who work underground in holes, caverns, and dark retirements, to conceal their mysteries from the eyes and observation of mankind. These subterraneous philosophers are daily employed in the transmutations of liquors, and by the power of magical drugs and incantations, raising under the streets of London the choicest products of the hills and valleys of France. They can squeeze Bordeaux out of the sloe, and draw Champagne from an apple. Virgil, in that remarkable prophecy,

'The ripening grape shall hang on every thorn'

seems to have hinted at this art, which can turn a plantation of northern hedges into a vineyard. These adepts are known among one another by the name of *Wine-brewers;* and, I am afraid, do great injury, not only to her Majesty's customs, but to the bodies of many of her good subjects." Modern industrial standardization notwithstanding, bottle for bottle American *ordinaire* is easily the most palatable the world produces today, and none of it is chemical counterfeit.

A more inspiring subject by far is the making of Champagne and sparkling wines generally. The classical method, *la méthode champenoise,* took over a century to develop and is still being refined today. The vintner begins by blending a *cuvée* (literally tubfull) of choice white wines. All Champagne is a blend, and the quality of the wines blended is the all-important factor: Champagne can be no better than the wine that's used. In France the only varieties employed are the Pinot Chardonnay and Pinot Noir (yes, a black grape). In California the *cuvée* usually contains others also, while most New York State and Ohio Champagne comes from *labrusca-*flavored varieties like Delaware and Catawba.

Champagne

Each vintner creates a blend of his own to constitute the *cuvée.* To the *cuvée* he adds a special Champagne yeast and about twenty pounds of

sugar for each one hundred gallons of wine. The yeast goes to work on the sugar, and the wine begins to ferment for a second time. It is bottled immediately, and the bottles are sealed with crown caps or with corks that are fastened down with steel clamps. They are stacked horizontally in tiers and left undisturbed for many months. This time the carbonic gas generated by fermentation has no way to escape. The bottles become bombs, the pressure often equalling a hundred pounds to the square inch. Finally the gas becomes a component of the wine itself and the wine becomes effervescent. It is now Champagne.

"secondary fermentation"

This secondary fermentation can take anywhere from a few weeks to a few months. It produces the much-prized bubbles, but it also produces a deposit of solid particles, dead yeast cells mainly, which are trapped in the bottle. To filter the wine would remove the sparkle along with the debris. Dom Pérignon, who is credited with the invention of Champagne while he was cellar master at the Benedictine Abby of Hautvillers from 1668 to 1715, never solved this problem. For over a hundred years people simply tried to ignore the sediment in their champagne. Finally a lady both fastidious and ingenious devised a way to get rid of it. The lady was a widow named Clicquot, who carried on her husband's Champagne business after his death and who invented the last steps in *la méthode champenoise.*

After the secondary fermentation is completed, the wine is allowed to age on the yeast sediment. The longer it ages, the more of the characteristic Champagne flavor and bouquet it develops. Then it's ready for "riddling," or as the French call it, *remuage* ("moving"). The idea is to dislodge the sediment from the sides of the bottle and get it to collect on the cap or cork. The bottles are stood with their necks down in special racks. Every day each bottle is given a short, sharp spin and dropped back into place. The

riddling

riddler or *remueur,* whose job this is eventually becomes skillful enough to give perhaps fifty bottles a minute just the right turn. The operation is extremely delicate, and the fate of each bottle rests literally on a flick of his wrist. As the riddling goes on, the angle at which the bottles are standing is gradually increased. This process may go on for two weeks or three months depending on the batch of wine. When all the sediment finally rests against the cap or cork and the wine is brilliantly clear, the neck of the bottle is thrust into a brine solution which freezes the sediment and perhaps an inch of wine. The bottle is then opened and the pressure expels the frozen plug. The sediment, thanks to Madame Clicquot's inspiration, is gone!

disgorging

Immediately after the disgorging, as this step is known, the *dosage* is added. *(Dosage,* like *remuage,* rhymes with garage. For obvious reasons, most Champagne terminology is borrowed from the French.) The *dosage* is a mixture of aged brandy, wine and sugar syrup with which each bottle is topped up. The amount of sugar in the *dosage* determines how the Champagne will be labelled. Even *brut,* the driest, contains a little; and *sec* has a little more. *Demi-sec* means approximately 5-percent and *doux* approximately 10-percent sugar. Despite a loss of carbon dioxide during disgorging, the pressure remains somewhere between thirty and sixty pounds to the square inch inside the bottle, so the final cork is wired down with good reason. By the time it's ready to be chilled and served, French Champagne is usually at least five years old, somewhat more mature than American, though produced with no more care. Regardless of where it comes from, each bottle of Champagne produced by *la méthode champenoise* requires an estimated one hundred twenty hand operations, and at least one in every one hundred blows up before completing its curriculum.

"dosage"

In unusually good years the French Champagne producers "declare a vintage"—otherwise their wines bear no vintage dates. The leading French firms include Ayala, Bollinger, Charles Heidsieck, Heidsieck Monopole, Henriot, Krug, Lanson, Moet & Chandon, Mumm, Perrier-Jouet, Piper Heidsieck, Pol Roger, Pommery et Greno, Louis Roederer and Veuve Clicquot. There are perhaps thirty such firms altogether, and you won't find much to complain about a bottle from any of them. Unfortunately, the same cannot be claimed for American Champagne producers, who actually outnumber the French. "Champagne," of course, is not simply another way of saying "white sparkling wine," and the French government has only grudgingly acquiesced to our using the name, since virtually no other country does. But language is not subject to legislation. Americans do call white sparkling wines "Champagne," and the snobbish practice of putting quotation marks around the word when applied to any other than French wine is just an exercise in self-importance. But since the same name is used for wines of different origins, comparisons are inevitable.

French producers

Nicholas Longworth of Cincinnati is the true father of New York Champagne. In 1845 he presented the world with 100,000 bottles of "Sparkling Catawba" made by the *méthode champenoise.* The most successful Eastern producers have continued to use both the time-honored techniques and the native-American *labrusca* grape varieties. The bubbly that results is as different from the taste of any other as a pear is from an apple, and just as good in its own right. The very driest New York Champagne is labelled *"brut* special," though some firms are content to label their driest simply *"brut."* "Special reserve" is midway between *"brut"* and "extra dry," which is actually the sweetest sold. The most highly regarded brand is probably Charles Fournier, followed by Gold Seal, Great Western, Taylor and Widmer.

New York Champagne

California Champagne

California's finest dry Champagnes are some of her finest products and deserve to rank with their French cousins among the great wines of the world. They share a family resemblance, but the California wines are great not because of any similarities but because of their own merits: great dryness, strong scent and comparatively forceful, straightforward flavors. To our way of thinking, these "very best" Champagnes come from Almadén, Beaulieu, Korbel, Hanns Kornell Champagne Cellars, Mirassou, Schramsberg and Weibel. (Almadén and Weibel also produce some that is less good, be it noted.) Beaulieu, Mirassou, and Schramsberg customarily vintage date their Champagnes, as does Almadén with its best, *Blanc de Blancs*.

Only white grapes go into the *cuvée* for a *Blanc de Blancs,* which is said to result somehow in a lighter Champagne. Jack Davies' Schramsberg produces the only other we know of (available through Neiman-Marcus and other selected outlets). As a virtuoso performance, Davies has also produced a *Blanc de Noirs,* a Champagne—white, of course—made exclusively from black grapes!

California Champagne labels can be especially puzzling. The critical factors making for fine Champagne quality are two: use of the finest varieties of grapes, and extended aging of the wine on its yeast sediment after secondary fermentation. The bottle labels will tell you nothing outright about either of these crucial elements. Your best guarantee of quality is the legend "fermented in this bottle"—not *the* but *this*. Hanns Kornell, Korbel, Mirassou and others in this way distinguish their products from those of companies using a simplified version of the *méthode champenoise*. Almadén and Paul Masson, among others, have developed a way to bypass the tedious riddling and disgorging stages in the Champagne process. Once secondary fermentation and aging are completed, a machine empties the bottles into a

pressurized tank. Under pressure of air or nitrogen the yeast and sediment are then filtered out and the wine, with the *dosage* added, is rebottled and corked. Champagne produced in this way is not nearly so effervescent—the bubbles are fewer and gone sooner—and is therefore less inspiring if only for this reason. It does undergo bottle fermentation and aging, however, so it is legally entitled to a "fermented in the bottle" label. As yet, the law has taken no notice of such little differences in method, which add up to the big difference between the passable and the best possible Champagne.

bulk process

Sparkling wines that bear the telltale words "bulk process" or "Charmat process" on their labels have little in common with any wines made by the *méthode champenoise*. They have no chance of being great and little chance of even being good. Most American Champagne, unfortunately, is produced in this much faster and cheaper way. The wine has a rapid secondary fermentation in glass or stainless-steel tanks, relatively small ones as wine tanks go, that hold from fifty to one thousand gallons. The sediment is either left behind in the tank or removed by filter when the wine is bottled, under pressure, with the *dosage.* So much sediment develops that the taste of the wine is ruined by any prolonged contact with it, but without a chance for extended aging on yeast sediment, the wine cannot approximate any Champagne flavor.

Unpleasantly yeasty, sour and raw are the kindest adjectives we can think of for the bulk-process Champagnes we have tried. The one use for such stuff might be in that unbelievable drink of the nineteenth-century Irish gentry, Black Velvet. Black Velvet consists of equal amounts of Champagne and good Guiness stout and is obviously of Irish origin, being designed to buckle the knees and cross your eyes for you. Bulk-process Champagne does not harm the flavor of the stout at all. Mimosas are also possible.

No sparkling wine is cheap, because the Federal tax on them is twenty times greater than the tax on still table wines. Since you have to pay the government such an excessive tariff for the bloody bubbles, doesn't it make sense to lay out a little more for a wine that's worth drinking around the bubbles?

Korbel and Mirassou put out the driest Champagnes, labeled respectively "natural" and *"au naturel,"* made with no sugar in the *dosage.* The other terms are *"brut,"* "extra dry," and "dry" (or *"sec"*), the sweetest of all, ironically. Excellent pink Champagnes are sometimes made by the *méthode champenoise,* but these, like sparkling Burgundy and lately Cold Duck, are for the most part bulk-process wines. Sparkling Burgundy is generally an inferior but pretty wine, popular with many non-wine drinkers who can't resist the combination of a certain sweetness and bubbles both in a red. Why anyone buys Cold Duck we cannot imagine, but they do, they do. Some twenty-five wineries now produce it.

Spanish Sherries

The most versatile and obliging of the fortified wines is Sherry, which takes its name from the Spanish town of Jerez de la Frontera, about one hundred twenty miles north of Gibraltar. The ancient name of the town was Xeres, and the Moors called it "Scherish." The region around Jerez produces not one or two or three, but dozens of different Sherries which may bear little or no resemblance to each other. The four most familiar imported types are: (1) *Fino.* Very dry, pale wine that may be served chilled as an aperitif or with food. Our favorites: Gonzales, Byass "Tio Pepe"; Pedro Domecq "La Ina"; Harvey's "Pale Dry Cocktail"; Duff Gordon's "Nina," "Pinta," and "Santa Maria." (2) *Amontillado.* Deeper in color, older, and somewhat more full-bodied than a *fino,* with a fragrance and lingering undertaste like toasted nuts. Our favorites: Duff Gordon "Amontillado";

Harvey's "Amontillado Pale Dry"; Sandeman's "Amontillado Fino." (3) *Dry Oloroso*. Very fragrant, full-bodied, and mellow. Our favorites: "Dry Sack"; Sandeman's "Dry Don"; Harvey's "Shooting Sherry"; Duff Gordon "No. 28"; Findlater, Mackie, Todd and Company's "Dry Fly." (4) *Dessert Oloroso*. Generally a dark golden amber, the richest and heaviest of Sherries. Our favorites: Harvey's "Bristol Cream"; Pedro Domecq's "Celebration Cream"; Duff Gordon's "Cream Sherry." There are numerous other Sherry shippers whose products, our friends assure us, are as good as any we have listed but these are the only ones for which we can speak from first-hand experience.

flor   There is at least three times as much California Sherry as there is Spanish, but the only ones which more or less approximate the original generally carry the words *flor* and/or *solera* on their labels. These refer not to kinds of Sherry but to the way it is made. Once the wine is fermented to dryness, wine spirits are added to bring the alcohol content up to about 15 percent and then the *flor* yeast is introduced into the mixture. *Flor* is Spanish for "flower," for it flowers into a thick scum atop the wine as it ages in open vats or casks. (For some reason, Spanish *olorosos* grow little or no *flor,* however.) Only in the last decade or so have California wineries begun using *flor* yeast in their Sherry making. After the wine is fully impregnated with the *flor* flavors, it is brought up to full alcoholic strength, somewhere between 18 and 21 percent, and then drawn off into casks.

solera   If the Sherry is made after the Spanish fashion, the casks are arranged into a *solera* system. A *solera* is basically a series of communicating barrels lying in superimposed rows four or five tiers high. The wine is not protected from the air but rather exposed to it, and to the contrasting heat of day and cool of night. Newer wine is always added to casks in the topmost tier of the *solera*. When the Sherry is judged fully mature and ready for bottling, just one-third to one-half a cask at a time is drawn off a bottom-tier cask. The bottom tier is replenished from the second row, and these in turn from the third, and so on. In its slow progress through the *solera* system, the new wine not only "marries" the old but also assumes its character. A remarkably small amount of old Sherry will "key" an enormous amount of young. This system of aging and blending enables a Sherry maker to market the same wine year after year because it all comes out of the same barrels. By the time it is withdrawn from a *solera,* the Sherry is a wonderfully harmonious and well-aged blend. Wineries that go to this much trouble to produce good Sherry usually use the Palomino grape from which Spanish Sherries are also made. The best California Sherries we've discovered come from Almadén, Brookside Vineyard, Llords & Elwood, Novitiate of Los Gatos and Weibel.

Names like *fino* or *oloroso* are not applied to California Sherry. "Cream" Sherry represents a California attempt at a dessert *oloroso,* the richest, sweetest sort. "Golden" usually denotes a somewhat drier, lighter-bodied wine. In descending order of dryness we then have "Sherry," "dry Sherry," "cocktail Sherry," and "pale dry Sherry." But every winery is allowed to juggle these names at will or to invent new ones, so occasionally a "cocktail Sherry" may be paler and drier than a "pale dry." If the label doesn't specify *flor* or *solera,* you must be guided by the winery's reputation. Beaulieu, Souverain, Heitz and Simi, to name a few we've tried, all produce (by whatever method) a fairly creditable Sherry.

If the winery has no reputation, you may assume you're merely buying a cheap, strong wine. Most of it is made by the so-called "baking" method. The basic wine is fermented to the desired degree of dryness, then spirits are added to check fermentation and preserve the remaining sugar

content. The wine is then kept for a number of months at around 120 degrees Fahrenheit in the hope that the resulting oxidation will make it taste like Sherry. It doesn't—though the best of these do rather resemble Madeira.

It is this fortification with alcohol to arrest fermentation of the grape sugar which is responsible for the greater alcoholic strength of aperitif and dessert wines generally. We have neither space not time, as the man who was put in a sack and drowned said, to account for the existence of Angelica, Madeira, Malaga, Marsala, Tokay and white Port. We've never encountered an American-made wine by these names we could recommend to anybody.

California Ports and Muscatels can be more rewarding. The best Ports seem to be produced from the Tinta Madeira grape. The Portuguese product generally makes California's version taste very bland, indelicate, and overly sweet in comparison. Ficklin, Paul Masson and the Noviate of Los Gatos, however, produce excellent Port, and prove by example that good California Port is at least possible. "Ruby" Port is younger and far redder than "tawny" Port, which has to be aged in the wood long enough to turn russet or almost brown. Muscat and Muscatel wines are among the sweetest and most ancient of all. They have a perfume and flavor unmistakably their own. Portugal, or more exactly the city of Setúbal in Portugal, is the leading producer of fine Muscat wines. The variety known as Muscat de Frontignan in France or Moscato di Canelli in Italy is the one that produces the most distinctive California Muscat wines. Bargetto, Beaulieu, Concannon, D'Agostini, Charles Krug and San Martin seem to do best by this distinctive family of grapes. "Muscatel" is only the most familiar of the several kinds of muscat wine made. There is also light-sweet Muscat, dry Muscat, cream of Muscat and sparkling Muscat. (Louis Martini's *Moscato Amabile* is one of California's truly unique wines; Hanns Kornell and Weibel also produce

fortification

Port

Muscats

distinguished sparkling Muscat. The prototype for them all is the excellent Italian *Asti Spumante.*) Anyone who aspires to try all the good things the earth provides should make the acquaintance of a good Muscat wine sometime. Many of them are not fortified.

No treatise on wine making can omit all mention of brandy. No doubt the most useful thing to know about it is how to make good old *brandy recipe* brandy out of positively vile stuff.

(1) Pour it through the air into a large receptacle—from the top of the stairs into a bathtub below, for instance.

(2) Put it into bottles, with a plum in each bottle.

(3) Stand it up with no corks in the bottles for some two or three days, even a week—or two or three weeks.

(4) Put a drop of maraschino into each bottle.

The bottles are now old brandy, and you can give them funny names and drink it out of big glasses and roll it around, warming it with your hands and smelling at it like a dog.

WINE HISTORY
How long has this been going on?

(A history of wine) . . . would need infinite research to satisfy my own ideas of thoroughness: for I have never yet given a second-hand opinion of anything or book or person. Also, I should have had to drink more good wine than would now be good for my pocket or perhaps even my health, and more bad than I could contemplate without dismay in my advancing years.

—George Saintsbury

entral heating and running water are not the only comforts the world forgot about when the Roman Empire collapsed beneath the onslaught of barbarian tribes. Lost also was that great comfort to the spirit, mature wine. There is no shortage of classical poets who testify in praise of wine, wine of every sort. One of the most difficult and endearing of them is Horace, the son of a slave who became the intimate of Augustus, the ruler of the world. His poems are devoid of snobbism; he's able to extol the Emperor's finest vintages and still invite him over for a bottle of *ordinaire* offered without apology.

wines of antiquity

Wine was plentiful in the ancient world and formed part of a slave's daily ration. The price for *ordinaire* in Rome over the years averaged about a dime per gallon. The better sorts of wine were put up in amphorae, which were then sealed, labelled and stored to age. Greek vintages reached maturity in about seven years; many of the Italian wines required twenty. As an aid to preservation the ancients often added turpentine or something similar—the Romans coated the insides of the amphora with pine pitch—to produce something on the order of retsina, which is the national wine of Greece to this day. But this was not the practice with all wines. The amphora, a porous pottery vessel stoppered with plaster or wax, allowed the wine to breathe and thus to go on getting better until it was as good as it could be.

"vappa"

When unresinated wine was inadequately preserved in the amphora— no unusual thing in ancient Italy—it turned to vinegar, and when vinegar exposed to the air lost its acidity, it became completely insipid. Such slop was called in Latin *vappa* (pronounced woppa) and the Romans used the word figuratively for any no-account person. This name for a good-for-nothing still persists in Neapolitan dialect and appears as "woppo." Applied years ago as a term of abuse by one New York Italian about another, it entered American slang as "wop," the standard racial slur flung at Italians.

Besides red and white the ancients had brown wine, which the world has done without very nicely ever since. Rich Romans of the first century A.D. had as large and varied a repetoire of wines to draw on as the wealthy have today, and the *nouveau riche* among them displayed the famous names and "right" years whenever they could obtain them. Trimalchio, for example, in that most fantastic of ancient stories, Petronius's *Satyricon*, claims to serve his guests the most notoriously expensive wine of the period. " 'Falernian from the year of Opimius's consulship, a hundred years in the bottle!' And as we were reading the labels, Trimalchio clapped his hands and cried, 'Alas that wine should live longer than wretched man! So let's wet our whistles for wine is life.' " The pretentious old Trimalchio was probably lying; Opimian vintage (121 B.C.) would actually have been much older. Pliny the Elder, who outlived Petronius thirteen years to perish with Pompeii, says: "There was such a blaze of hot weather that in that year the grapes were literally cooked—cooking is the technical word—by the sun and the wines made last to this day after nearly two hundred years."

ancient connoisseurship

Two hundred and fifty years after the last Emperor stepped down from his throne, his realms had been divided between the Christian Pope in the West and the Islamic Caliph in the East. Their opposing views were almost equally barren: the Moslem practice favored plenty of women but absolutely no wine, whereas the Catholic ideal permitted plenty of wine but no women. The Dark Ages are rightly so-called. Life might have proved altogether impossible in Europe but for the late Roman invention of the barrel. Wooden barrel staves must be exactly coopered so as to fit together

barbarism and the barrel

115

and bent so that pressure is exerted equally throughout. Then the heads must be fitted such that the whole is proof against leakage—no mean engineering achievement. People would sometimes put wine in jugs stopped up with straw and with a layer of olive oil on top of it to protect it from the air, but mainly they kept their wine in barrels. The wine had to be drunk quickly, before it had a chance to turn to vinegar, which it often did even before the next year's vintage was in. There was a perennial shortage of wine, and the scholarly medieval poets, with a combination of thirst and piety, constantly besought their patrons for supplies when they ran out of wine and bitter beer raged in their bellies.

As the feudal period drew to its unlamented end, the trade in wine picked up. Quality was never high, perhaps, by modern (or ancient) standards, but people learned to distinguish different regional wines and merchants learned to fool their customers. Climatic changes had rendered England unfit for grape growing, though the Romans had pursued viticulture successfully there. Forced to import their wines, the English became more sophisticated wine drinkers than their contemporaries who were able to satisfy themselves with home production. Chaucer has his Pardoner, a confessed beer drinker, begin his tale

*a Chaucerian
admonition*

> Now keep ye from the white and from the red,
> And namely from the white wine of Lepe,
> That is to sell in Fish Street or in Chepe.
> This wine of Spain creepeth subtilly
> In other wines, growing fast by,
> Of which there riseth such fumositee,
> That when a man has drunken draughtes three
> And weneth that he be at home in Chepe,
> He is in Spain, right at the town of Lepe,
> Not at the Rochelle nor at Bordeaux town.

Lepe, the modern Niebla located not far from Seville, evidently produced a strong cheap wine which was sold under its own name in Chaucer's London and which was also used for adulterating better wines from Bordeaux and La Rochelle. Its "fumositee"—delightful word!—found its way into the weaker French wines and got you drunk the quicker. The fumes of the wine then transported the inebriate not to Bordeaux or La Rochelle where they supposedly came from but to Lepe, the home of the strong wine predominant in the mixture. The Middle Ages and Renaissance added all manner of honey and herbs to their wines to mask their defects and render them potable, and the sweeter the wine, the more it was valued in those cold and sugarless days. A young Beaujolais or rosé will give some idea of the very best unadulterated wine most men of those times could hope to come by, and that not too often.

"Clairette"

The chief source of England's beverage continued for three hundred years to be Bordeaux. The generally mediocre quality of this short-lived and light-colored wine is obvious from its name *Clairette,* which the English with their sovereign disdain for other people's spelling called Claret. All this was changed about the beginning of the eighteenth century when England, being on the outs with the aged Louis Quatorze, concluded a treaty with the Portuguese whereby their wines could enter Britain paying a much lower import duty than the French. The only difficulty English policy and the Portuguese merchants encountered came from the wine itself. So horribly harsh and dry was it, no Englishman wanted to buy it at any price. The

Port and fortification

merchants at Oporto learned to fortify their product with brandy and thus to check fermentation and retain in the wine sufficient sugar to make it palatable. This expedient was discovered and first put into practice sometime between 1725 and 1730, but more was needed. The wine and alcohol required time to amalgamate and throw off impurities. The solution was a second stroke of genius: bottling the wine and corking the bottles.

But to give honor where it's due, we must backtrack a bit and mention Dom Pérignon, supposedly the very first to hit upon the cork-and-bottle idea. "Come quickly," the blind monk is supposed to have cried, "I'm drinking stars." He had invented Champagne. Grapes ripen slowly in the Champagne district and must be harvested late. Having a fairly low sugar content, they also ferment slowly. The winter cold arrests the fermentation process until springtime warms the wine, and it begins to ferment again. Dom Pérignon blended the wines from his neighborhood and then bottled the blend as it began to undergo its secondary fermentation. The gas given off by fermentation had to remain dissolved in the wine, awaiting release in the form of bubbles once the bottle was uncorked. Most of the good monk's bottles exploded, of course, and another century had to pass before somebody found a way to get the sediment out of the Champagne. Sparkling wine, therefore, only became fashionable and widely known long after Port. When Dom Pérignon departed this vale of tears in 1715, he left it immeasureably happier and richer, not only for Champagne but also for the cork, which the purveyors of Port were so soon to popularize.

"that was a very good year"

This is a fitting point in our story to give thanks for this "most important event in the history of fine wine," the invention of the cork. Wine, as we have seen, requires air to stay alive. But there comes a point when wine left in the wood begins to oxidize too fast, to "burn up." In its cask it would become emaciated and tired long before reaching maturity. Put in a bottle and allowed no more air than seeps through a cork, good wine goes on improving slowly until it achieves the fulfillment of all its innate potential. When next you get the chance to enjoy a fine wine, properly aged, reflect that this is a pleasure mankind did without for fifteen hundred years until we came up with an equivalent to the classical stoppered amphora.

the invention of the cork

The cork revolutionized the drinking and appreciation of wine in the course of the eighteenth century. Watteau's paintings show that wine in the bottle was known at the French Court by the time of his death in 1727. And a few among the British aristocracy began to appreciate the fine points in the wines becoming available to them, as the copious correspondence of those pre-telephone days will testify. One Lord Carlisle writes George Augustus

Selwyn, one of society's trend setters at the time: "I wish you would speak to Foxcroft in case he should have a pipe of exceeding good Claret, to save it for me. I do not mean that you shall have anything to do with choosing it for me, for you can drink ink and water if you are told it is Claret. Get somebody who understands it to taste it for you." Only the wealthy could afford to cultivate a taste for Claret or the other French wines in that period. The reasonably priced beverage wines were not French. Rhine wines gained *18th century tastes* great popularity, and since much of it was shipped from Hochheimer, national habit compelled the English to call all Rhine wine "Hock." But the eighteenth century was not a time of delicacy and refinement, and though they were fond of wine, often disastrously so, most people were far more concerned with quantity than with quality, and took more interest in the kick the wine promised than its more subtle and artistic aspects. The spirit of the time is apparent in a song from Sheridan's *School for Scandal* which we like well enough to quote.

> Here's to the maiden of bashful fifteen,
> Now to the widow of fifty;
> Here's to the flaunting extravagant queen,
> And here's to the housewife that's thrifty.
>   Let the toast pass—drink to the lass!
>   I warrant she'll prove an excuse for the glass.

The song goes on proposing toasts for four more stanzas, with always the same refrain.

For the English it was pre-eminently the Age of Port. Horace Walpole, the foremost letter writer of his day, refers nowhere in his corres- *The Age of Port* pondence to a château or vintage year but mentions Port constantly. He writes, for instance, that doctors were much impressed by the case of Charles

Mildmay, Lord Fitzwalter, who was still alive in December, 1755. He was past eighty-four, had been a great ladies' man and, according to Horace, "had scarce ever more sense than he has at present." For many months he had been thriving on fourteen barrels of oysters, seven bottles of brandy, and two-dozen bottles of Port a week.

Lo! The nineteenth century—the Golden Age of Wine the English call it. In the ninety-nine years between the day Napoleon retired in defeat from the field of Waterloo and that on which German forces struck across Belgium at France, Europe knew no general war. Uprisings aplenty, but these were local matters. The Crimean and Franco-Prussian conflicts were self-contained and neatly concluded bloodbaths that did little more than give the bourgeoisie at home something diverting to discuss. And with the growth of industrialism they were meantime making more and more money and spending more and more of it on wines. Even the not-so-wealthy had space and time to lay down bottles for twenty or thirty years. The Russian troops opposing Napoleon in the Waterloo campaign had been quartered in Champagne. They plundered all the cellars of the district and carried an unquenchable thirst for Champagne back home with them to the steppes. The fashion gradually spread to other countries too, but the Champagne merchants recovered far more than their losses from the Russian market alone over the century that ensued.

Champagne

Claret was once again the standard wine of Englishmen. Everyone with any pretention to social standing affected connoisseurship. The Bordeaux *châteaux* became name brands, and it was mainly to publicize the Bordeaux wines—and to enhance their snob appeal—that their wily French promoters devised the notorious "Classification of 1855." The Bordeaux Chamber of Commerce commissioned a group of brokers to draw up a list of

Classification of 1855

the best vineyards to represent the region at the Universal Exhibition in Paris. They came up with sixty-five *châteaux*—as even the most modest of Bordeaux wineries may be called—which they ranked in five categories or "growths." This classification has probably done more to swell the ranks of the wine snobs than anything before or since. The classification was based on price and intended to single out the wines which had, on the average, commanded the highest prices up to that time. From then 'til now the Bordeaux merchants and exporters have been able to exploit the reputation of these these "growths" or *crus,* and thus they have remained the most expensive. Although the experts responsible for the classification emphasized that it was provisional and would go out of date, their list has in no way been altered.

les crus

By the middle of the century, more wine was being produced—and more being aged—than ever before in Europe. According to educated estimates, at least 25 percent of it spoiled before completing fermentation, but much of what survived must have been extraordinary. The Victorians seldom spoke in superlatives except when it came to the wines they loved. The wine trade was thus at its zenith in Europe by the time another chapter in wine history was well underway in the New World.

From the very first days of colonization the Spaniards took the grapevine with them everywhere they went in the New World. Cortés himself established this grape growing policy in Mexico, probably to insure that there would always be wine enough for the mass to be celebrated. Thus when Father Junipero Serra in 1769 founded at San Diego the first of the missions he was to establish in California, obedient to Spain's policy and mindful of the church's needs, he planted California's first grapevines there. The "Mission" grape is still grown in California and probably today produces

"Mission" wine

no worse wine than it did back then. Those early Spanish had probably found this variety growing in Sardinia (where it grows to this day), and chose it because it was easily transplanted and hardy enough to survive anywhere. And survive it did, at every one of the missions where it was planted, being made into both wine of a sort and brandy, as old mission records show: "Father Duran at Santa Barbara made aguardiente as clear as crystal, or when treated with burnt sugar, of a clear yellow. It was doubly distilled and as strong as the reverend father's faith."

first Californian vintner

In 1823, the year the last of the missions was founded in Sonoma, Joseph Chapman in Los Angeles became the first Californian to seek a livelihood raising grapes and selling wine. Chapman, the Yankee entrepreneur and a one-time pirate, soon had a competitor in the person of Jean-Louis Vignes, a cooper from Bordeaux who brought with him the first French vines to grace the soil of California. The appropriately named Vignes established El Aliso, his ranch and vineyard, in the heart of present-day Los Angeles; by 1840 he was able to ship quantities of dry white wine and of aguardiente to San Francisco. (His prices were outrageous: two dollars and four dollars the gallon, respectively.)

Don Benito Wilson

" . . . and in 1841 appeared Benjamin Davis Wilson, a Tennessean in a fringed jacket, who instantly took to the milieu, planted his acres, and became Don Benito, one with the grandees. The transplantation was a happy one; he throve like the indigenous toyon-bush, became more Spaniard than the natives, grew fair wine, less good than Don Luis Vignes' claret, bought ranch after ranch, and hacked a road up a mountain that he admired, and a convenience it was for the astronomers who later built their Mt. Wilson telescope upon it. His land was Oak Knoll, the site now of the Huntington Library at San Marino. Don Benito became the first mayor of Los Angeles,

and the last, they say, to know the grape, and on pouring a bottle to utter in the Spanish way a prayer to the vine-dressers whose care made it a wine worth pouring."

So runs the account given by Idwal Jones, stylist *extraordinaire,* and it is to his *Vines in the Sun* you must turn for a complete (and completely entertaining) history of the wines and vines of California before 1900. But not even so short a synopsis of that fascinating history as this one can dismiss in a few lines the career of Agoston Haraszthy, visionary and adventurer. Should you wonder how a Hungarian nobleman came to be devoured by alligators in Nicaragua in 1869, you will allow us a long enough digression to tell his story.

Agoston Haraszthy

Haraszthy had given up his hereditary title of count for the more democratic one of colonel before he set out for California at the head of a wagon train in 1849. His destination, however, was not the gold fields of the north but rather San Diego where he thought to find the best land for winegrowing. Vineyards had kept the Haraszthys wealthy for centuries in Hungary, but Agoston had been forced to flee his native soil when the popular uprising in which he played a role had collapsed and the reactionary government placed a price on his head. With characteristic decisiveness he straightway betook himself and his family to the New World and established a town in Wisconsin named, with characteristic modesty, for himself. His interests prospered—the real estate and steamboat concerns, the farms where he raised Wisconsin's first field of hops and first flock of sheep. Only the vineyard failed so he left what was to become Sauk City behind him and made for San Diego, then a town whose population approached seven hundred on Sundays. Getting himself elected sheriff almost at once, Haraszthy became judge and then state assemblyman before the vines on his farm had a chance to bear their first fruit. The new assemblyman soon moved the family to a new farm, Las Flores, located near San Francisco's Mission Dolores and went to work setting out more vines imported from Europe.

It was in February of 1852 that Haraszthy received a couple of bundles of cuttings he could not identify. The label, which he deciphered with difficulty, seemed to read "Zinfandel." Frank Schoonmaker has written " . . . if an absence of apparent ancestors is proof of divine origin certainly the Zinfandel grape is entitled to a whole collection of legends. Ampelographers have been able to arrive at any number of negative conclusions about it: the Zinfandel is *not* the German Zierfandler, it is not, as was long believed, the Hungarian Kadarka, it was *not* brought over from Europe under this name (Zinfandel)." And it is not found anywhere else in the world except in California. Though seldom large the vine is productive and its clusters are so compact that the grapes in the center of the bunch are sometimes crushed. Zinfandel has been called California's own Beaujolais, and many among us find in it every virtue a wine should have. In popularity and sheer quantity of production, there is today no grape to rival it in the state. The good Colonel H. was never to know what a boon he had conferred upon his adopted land.

the Zinfandel

The Colonel seems to have restricted himself to strictly legal methods in his energetic efforts to raise capital. That at least was the conclusion of the courts after numerous trials, appeals and retrials in which Haraszthy was charged with embezzlement in connection with his stint as head of the San Francisco Mint. The lawsuits dragged on longer than the job had lasted, but neither political appointment nor public scandal diverted much of his attention from the acquisition of land and the planting of vines. Eventually

Buena Vista

he owned the world's largest vineyard, six thousand acres of choice Sonoma countryside that he named Buena Vista. He built his family a fabulous Pompeian villa, entertained his distinguished neighbors, wrote a *Report on the Grapes and Wines of California* to please the State Agricultural Society, sent one of his sons to France to learn Champagne making and won prizes for his wines continuously at the State Fairs. Whereas other farmers employed Indian labor, Haraszthy brought one hundred and fifty Chinese up from San Francisco to work his vast holdings. They excavated deeper and deeper tunnels to be used as wine cellars and used the rock to build more stone vat houses for fermentation. Often when the heat of the day had been too oppressive, the pigtailed workmen could be seen plowing and dressing the vines in silence by the light of the moon.

grape gathering

By 1861 Haraszthy's prestige was such that the state legislature selected him to go to Europe to collect cuttings of vines and to learn all that he could about viticulture and the making of wines to make it common knowledge in California. He left on his mission in June of that year and visited France, Italy, Switzerland, Spain and then Germany. At Johannisberg he confessed to Prince Metternich that his Excellency's Riesling was "of a perfection that as yet had no California peer." He brought back, in addition to his bales of notes, a dozen cart loads of fruit and nut trees and at least 200,000 cuttings of every imaginable sort of vine for the state to distribute for free throughout all the counties. All this work of collecting cost the Colonel nearly a year and twelve thousand dollars out of his own pocket. Because of his pro-Southern politics, however, the Legislature reneged on its promise to reimburse him and rejected the plants he'd gathered and the report he'd prepared as well. In 1946 the state set up a plaque commemorating Haraszthy's work; that is all the payment he ever received. He tried to distribute the vines himself. He envisioned California as the vineyard of the globe, a real utopia flowing with wine and honey, pheasant practically falling from the sky and casks of Zinfandel in every man's cellar. But he found it harder and harder to communicate this vision, and his projects began to fail.

He lost Buena Vista and then nearly lost his life when a boiler he was inspecting in his son's brandy distillery exploded practically in his face. At last he gave up the idea of re-establishing the Haraszthys in their noble and hereditary role of wine producers. His last venture was a sugar plantation in Nicaragua where he settled in 1869. Perhaps he intended to return to his beloved California where his sons carried on his name, but it was fated otherwise. One summer morning he left his house to search out a good site for a lumber mill and simply disappeared. It's claimed he was tracked as far as a large magnolia tree overhanging a stream whose waters were boiling with alligators. The trail is said to have ended there, causing his people to figure he'd fallen in trying to get across. Who knows? "He who plants a vine becomes entangled in its branches," wrote Flaubert we forget just where. Agoston Haraszthy, Count or Colonel, is only of historical interest to lovers of California's wine today (although there are still some convinced that thousands of ideally aged bottles of California's finest are waiting to be discovered when the hillside tunnels which collapsed during the 1906 tremor are completely excavated.) More than any man, he managed to adapt the technique of the Old World vineyards and wine masters to the untested climate and virgin soil of California. His monument is the Zinfandel. More than anyone else, it is Haraszthy California must thank for its present-day position in the world of wine.

Less than a century after his death, California could already boast more than twenty thousand active vineyards and around two hundred and

"what a fall . . . "

the legacy

forty commercial wineries. Few counties in the state have no winery at all, though Yolo has never had but one. The Napa-Sonoma and Santa Clara regions harbor twenty-eight or more apiece, and there are only a few less in San Bernardino. Fresno County has more than twenty; Stanislaus and San Joaquin more than thirty. Together these wineries account for approximately 6 percent of the world's annual wine production.

By the time of Haraszthy's unheralded death, a scourge had descended on the wine lands of the Old and New Worlds alike. In Portugal it first appeared in 1868; by the following year it had reached Bordeaux; it spread swiftly everywhere. By the mid-1870's European wine production had fallen off at least 50 percent, and it must have seemed that wine would soon be only a memory. The tiny aphid-type insects devouring the roots of the vines resisted every conceivable remedy. The *Phylloxera* had come from America and so, eventually, did the cure in the form of native American vine stocks which were found to be immune to the root louse. The devastation was unparalleled in agricultural history and required incredible toil to repair. Virtually all the vines of the world have been grafted on to the roots of native American grapes ever since and *Phylloxera* is all but unknown today. The threat persisted, however, until 1971, when University of California scientists announced a new way of preventing *Phylloxera* which does not necessitate the time and toil of grafting.

Phylloxera

California suffered somewhat less damage than the other wine lands from the *Phylloxera;* it was the hand of man that nearly put an end to wine production in this country. The "Noble Experiment" Prohibition went into effect in 1919 and for fourteen years thereafter a legal drought lay upon the land. The authorities permitted a handful of wineries to continue to operate making altar wines; Concannon and Beaulieu were among the fortunate few.

"The Noble Experiment"

131

The law also allowed home production of up to two hundred gallons of wine per annum, and most vineyards were reduced to shipping their grapes East to satisfy this demand. The better varieties of wine grape did not withstand the rigors of shipment, being thin-skinned and fragile. Fine wine grapes are, in any case, attractive neither to the mouth nor the eye of any but a vine-yardist, and so the Rieslings, Cabernets, Pinots and others were uprooted and replaced by the high-yielding mediocre types like Carignane, Thompson *the costs* Seedless and Alicante Bouschet. In 1929 some eight hundred carloads of this potential California red were shipped from Napa County alone. Since the profession of making wine was outlawed, the men who did it were forced into other fields. The tanks and casks that grow more precious with time and are the pride of the vintner's heart were sold or abandoned to a long and sad emptiness which few survived. Dry rot and the spider ruled the wineries undisturbed, except by an occasional roar like the roll of artillery as the irreplaceable cooperage collapsed. Worst of all was the effect of Prohibition on the public's taste. By 1930 America was consuming about 140,000 gallons of domestic "wine" per year, according to the estimates of the government's dry enforcement bureau. This was nearly twice the amount of wine that all the grapes in the country could have produced! Bootleggers had learned to make as much as six or seven hundred gallons of "wine" from a single ton of grapes by fermenting sugar and water on the skins after they had already been pressed dry. The stuff was red, alcoholic and available: people forgot how good wine tasted.

The wreckage of the wine industry that Prohibition wrought required not years but decades to repair. Quality wines could not be produced until the vineyards had been replanted, new cooperage acquired, and experienced winemakers found. Even after good and occasionally fine domestic wines became available, it was years and years before enough consumers acquired the critical experience necessary to care what they were drinking and create a market for quality. Except for the war years, the wine industry throughout the nation was far from prosperous until 1960 or so. Prohibition was really an experiment in barbarism. Incarnate civilization, and its blood would be wine. No liquid flows more incessantly through the labyrinth of symbols we have conceived to mark our status as human beings.

modern barbarity

   We have other forms of prohibition now, but hopefully Americans will not be prohibited wine, at least, again. But what are the prospects for good wine, what is the future of fine wine in this country? Speaking of the California wine industry in his book, *Wines and Spirits,* Mr. Alex Waugh wonders if there's any sound business reason why, with everything going so well, the hunt for those rare places that can produce exceptional vintages should continue. The omnibibulous Mr. Waugh should be relieved to learn that extensive prospecting for new vineyards is not only in progress but has begun to pay off. Wines from Lake, Monterey or San Benito counties may someday command the same respect that is today accorded those of the Napa and Livermore valleys. "It may take us a hundred years to find out where these vines should be planted in California," wrote Colonel Haraszthy in the report he presented along with the grape cuttings he brought back from Europe. His estimate was optimistic. It took much longer than that for Spain to find its lone Sherry region or for France to locate its Clos de Vougeot. It may be several centuries yet before the Californian *terroir* is exhaustively prospected. All the new plantings have heavily favored the best varieties of grapes. Whereas there were less than five hundred acres of Pinot

a good question

prospecting

133

Chardonnay in the entire state until fairly recently, today Almadén alone has nearly fifteen hundred acres of this noble grape either planted or projected.

Much of this expansion has unfortunately been necessitated by urban sprawl in the Bay Area. Some of the best white-wine vineyards on earth have been given over to tract housing in the Livermore Valley and the Napa district is similarly threatened. The Concannons have insured their permanent residency in the Livermore Valley by protecting their invaluable vineyards under California's Land Conservation Act, which provides that their property will continue to be assessed for taxes at its agricultural value only, even if the neighboring land owners discover gold. Hopefully, other vineyards will want to follow their example before it's too late.

The major factor prompting this expansion of vineyard acreage, however, has been the unprecedented boom in wine sales. In 1960 fortified dessert wines of the cheapest sort accounted for more than half of all the wine sold in the United States. Their sales since then have declined by 15 percent, while our consumption of dry table wines has nearly tripled in the same period. Well over half the total volume sold today is table wine: for the first time in this country, wine bibbers outnumber the winos! In 1970 Americans consumed some 70 percent more wine than in 1960, a record 267 million gallons. Approximately 11 percent of this total was imported, but the annual increase in imports is dwarfed by the growth of our domestic production. California's production of table wines has increased nearly 60 percent since 1964!

corporate invaders   The wine boom has not been an unmixed blessing, however: every year the list of corporate- or conglomorate-owned wineries gets longer and longer. Seagram has a stake in Paul Masson and Christian Brothers. National Distillers owns Almadén. Beaulieu and Inglenook belong to Heublein now,

and Nestlé recently acquired Beringer. There are other examples also. Even the uncynical will find it hard to believe that Big Business can have a salutary effect on the policies and production of our premium wineries. As long as Messrs. Maynard Monaghan and André Tchelistcheff preside over the destiny of Beaulieu we can be sure there will be no slippage in the standards of that "California château with a name for its wines as great as it is justified," to quote Mr. John Melville. But the alarmists are no longer alone in fearing the eclipse, if not the demise, of the family-owned winemaking operation with generations-old traditions of excellence. Fine wine can never be mass-produced. Fine wine, like any creative art work, is the result of individual skill and applied talent. Can the corporations accept the fact that wine is a personal, indeed a temperamental, product to produce? *"Vedremo in cento anni,"* as the Italians say when setting out a vine: "We'll see in a hundred years." We'll see much sooner in this case. It is also to be hoped that the *new wineries* future will confirm the promise shown by such recently established wineries as Chalone, Oakville Vineyards, Trentadue and ZD Wines—all names that the wine bibber will want to keep an eye out for.

Wine politics is another factor affecting the quality of the wines to come. Will state laws regulating varietal labelling be improved? Will Congress *ever* understand the wisdom behind Thomas Jefferson's words, "I think it is a great error to consider a heavy tax on wines, as a tax on luxury"?

Lastly, we must take into account the price and promises of technology. Professor Amerine and his justly renowned colleagues in the Department of Viticulture and Enology at the University of California, Davis, have perforce placed their knowledge and facilities at the disposal of the wine industry as a whole. The labels naming the grape cuttings good old Colonel Haraszthy imported were subsequently lost or mixed up. The professors are still at work straightening out the confusion. Some years back they had to inform one vineyard owner that his prize-winning Johannisberg Riesling was actually a little-known variety called Red Veltliner. They have also come up with hybrid varieties like Emerald Riesling, from which Paul Masson and San Martin have produced wine of some quality, and Ruby Cabernet. A third hybrid, a cross between Semillon and Traminer grapes, is called Flora and was just recently bottled as a varietal for the first time, we are told, by Souverain Cellars. The one bottle we have tasted was as fragrant as wood violets and excellent in every respect. But for all its contributions, the multiversity is of necessity morally neutral, so to speak. Its technological ingenuity and experimental expertise aid the industry in developing premium wines that require little aging and stay perfectly brilliant and free of sediment. Giving the public what it demands is doubtless good for profits, but is it also good for quality? Fine wine, which should be a living thing, is often machine filtered and "polished" to death by vintners who fear that a single speck of natural sediment, which is only a sign of the wine's age and health, might offend the customer's eye.

enological innovations

God knows the new methods and shiny equipment are not all bad. Technology has recently made possible a major advance in the art of making wine. We are indebted to Mr. Daniel Mirassou for calling to our attention an invention which will, as he said, affect "the future of quality in wine today." In 1969 the Mirassous experimented with a machine which is a grape harvester and crusher and tank truck all in one. Within a few seconds the grape has been stemmed and crushed and the juice stored in tanks and blanketed by carbon-dioxide gas. There is no pump, nothing to aerate or beat the liquid or in any way injure it. It is completely unaffected by the carbon-dioxide gas protecting it from the air. When the harvester tanks are

capturing the fragrance

full, the carbon-dioxide pressure is increased and it gently pushes the must out into a tank truck. The wine produced was so remarkable that the Mirassous field-crushed their entire crop of Chenin Blanc in 1970. The inventor, Wallace Johnson of Up-Right Harvesters has realized his ambition to make possible a wine whose hypothetical label could read: "The exceptional quality of this wine results from superior grapes picked at the peak of ripeness at a predawn coolness of 60 degrees. The full flavor of each grape is preserved by instant conversion into juice, protected fermentation and careful aging. The first time this wine (or the juice from which it is fermented) is in contact with air is the moment that you uncork this bottle and allow the wine to release its fragrance." We have tried Mirassou's dramatic Chenin Blanc and agree completely with their conclusion: they have captured all the fragrance of the grape!

*the quality of
a man's wine*

The impact of this invention remains to be seen. But any winemaster can attest to the truth which Peter Mondavi, one of the scions of Charles Krug, has stated: "To make outstanding wines a vintner should maintain a balance between the introduction of modern equipment and the need to maintain the human element. Old timers believe the quality of a man's wine depends on his own quality and character, a little bit of himself going into every bottle. To gain lasting fame he has to be a poet, a philosopher and an honorable man as well as a master craftsman." Our best assurance of the future of quality in wine rests with the earth itself, which ennobles those who work it: the soil is on the side of nobility. Truly fine wines will always be scarce, but old Bacchus and his colleague St. Vincent, the patron saint of wine and wine making, will see to it there's a supply. Future generations will not wonder why we say: "Wine is one of life's few absolutely reliable pleasures."

WINE VARIETIES
What are we drinking anyhow?

There are Thasian vines, there are white Mareotic;
The first thrive on fat terroir, the second on poorer soil.
Also there's the Psithian, useful in raisin wines, and
Light Lagean, someday sure to trip and tongue-tie you.
And Purple and Precian and you, Rhaetian, how
Am I to bottle your poetry?
Compare yourself not with finest Falernian though!
From Aminnean vines come the soundest of wines
Which Tmolian and even the kingly Chian bow before;
There's the minor Argitis which surpasses all others
Alike in yield of juice and length of life.
Nor shall I pass you by, vine of Rhodes,
Prized by banqueting men and gods with the second course
Nor, Bumastis, you with your swelling clusters.
There is no number for the many kinds
And names of wines there are . . . .

—Virgil

California's North Coastal Wine Country

Napa

1 Fetzer
2 Parducci
3 Italian Swiss
4 Pedroncelli
5 Trentadue
6 Cambiaso
7 Simi
8 Windsor Vineyards
9 Korbel
10 Russian River Vineyards
11 Buena Vista
12 Hanzell
13 Sebastiani
14 ZD Wines
15 Cuvaison
16 Schramsberg
17 Charles Krug
18 Freemark Abbey
19 Christian Brothers
20 Heitz
21 Hanns Kornell
22 Louis M. Martini
23 Souverain
24 Stony Hill
25 Beringer
26 Sutter Home Winery
27 Beaulieu
28 Inglenook
29 Robert Mondavi
30 Oakville Vineyards
31 Mayacamas
32 Christian Brothers
33 Wooden Valley
34 Concannon
35 Cresta Blanca
36 Wente Brothers
37 Weibel
38 Ridge
39 Llords & Elwood
40 Paul Masson
41 Martin Ray
42 Novitiate of Los Gatos
43 Pedrizetti
44 Emilio Guglielmo
45 San Martin
46 Fortino Brothers
47 Bargetto
48 Almadén
49 Almadén
50 Mirassou
51 Chalone

California

his chapter will be unfair, misleading and unabashedly prejudiced—and for this we will offer no apologies. We have been tasting and drinking California wines attentively for over six years. We had, by the time we met, each of us accumulated cellar books of a sort containing some note or record of over a thousand wines apiece. We have tried to sort out our experience and have deliberated deeply trying to discover which brands we do and would prefer in each category of wine. Our choices represent intensely personal appreciations and the brands listed are, with few exceptions, mutually agreed upon. No doubt we have sometimes drawn distinctions where no differences exist, and this is only one of our shortcomings. Omitting any mention of over half the wineries in California is manifestly unfair; random samplings and memories are notoriously misleading; our prejudices will not stay in hiding. Nevertheless we hope this chapter will be more useful than an historical document recording judgments of certain vintages of certain varietals from certain wineries. Such a book goes out of date before it gets into print. Not only have most of the wines considered disappeared from the merchants' shelves, but the ones remaining will have gotten better or worse in the interim, for wines and human beings never stay the same.

One is always reduced to generalizations in discussing wines and there is always an element of risk in choosing them. Every wine bibber has discoveries, surprises and disappointments to tell about, and this is the record of ours thus far. The wines we list as personal favorites we have found by experience to be consistently outstanding as compared with all the others we know. Inevitably, these are the ones we drink most often and know best, but every wine we mention has been tried more than once and very few less than three or four times. Please understand that our judgments are not definitive but tentative appraisals of quality. We look forward to many more hours of vinous *volupté* and reserve the right to change our minds. We are content, meanwhile, to be known by the fruit of our experience, which is necessarily dependant upon a mathematical factor. There are only fourteen meals in the week and there is a limit to how much one can drink at any meal. We have done our utmost considering the sacrifice of sobriety required! We feel that Californian Sherry, Champagne and Port can be evaluated only in comparison with their European prototypes and in terms of the ways they are made; our preferred brands have therefore been listed in the chapter on winemaking.

PINOT CHARDONNAY
[Pee-no´ Shar´-doe-nay]

Pinot Chardonnay is a glorious grape. It is cultivated most extensively in Burgundy and the tiny Chablis area in France, where it produces white wines you would sell your soul for. In Champagne to the north it is grown along with Pinot Noir for use in Champagne, and around Mâcon to the South it produces that fine wine, Pouilly-Fuissé. It may have been raised by the Romans in all of these districts. The aristocratic Chardonnay is one of the three or four grapes capable of producing truly great white wines in California. Though a full-bodied wine with a pungent perfume, it has the delicacy of crystal and is smooth as frog's fur in the mouth. People speak of it as having an "apple-like" aroma, but we have found this not always the case. You can, however, almost invariably detect the flavors of the oak in which it was aged. The taste is characterized by great finesse and roundness and a very balanced and appetizing dryness. The vine yields very grudgingly and the wine is accordingly expensive; in California, as in France, it is also used in Champagne. Perhaps two out of every three Chardonnays of the first rank that we have found have come from Napa-Sonoma wineries, but fortunately no single region has a monopoly. It should only escort foods of gourmet quality and is especially good with lobster or cracked crab and seafood generally. It can even be used as the one wine with a carefully planned buffet, for we have found it enhances chicken, turkey, cold meats, lamb and even ham when you're in the mood for something white, excellent and chilled.

Pinot Chardonnay suffers when blended very much, so it is important to look for the words "estate-bottled" or a vintage year. Every year since 1965 we have had at least two great bottles of Chardonnay from each of the following wineries: Beaulieu ("Beaufort"), Buena Vista, Charles Krug, Hanzell (heavenly!), Heitz Cellar (remarkably reliable), Martin Ray (stalwart and of exceedingly rare beauty), Mayacamas, Mirassou, Stony Hill and Wente.

Our second-echelon favorites are hardly less distinguished. These also have rewarded us with some great and many near-great bottles over the years, but the quality of the wine or our own luck has been less consistent with: Almadén, Christian Brothers, Inglenook, Llords & Elwood, Louis M. Martini (excellent except when not), San Martin, Sebastiani and Weibel.

It should be noted that the vintage and estate-bottled notations in the cases of Almadén and Weibel respectively seem to us to indicate no higher quality. We have also had potentially great Chardonnays produced by: Chalone Vineyards, Cuvaison, Freemark Abbey, Robert Mondavi and Ridge Vineyards. Their exceptional wines have been available only a few years, however, and it will be a few years yet before we know where they rank. Pinot Chardonnay ages beautifully, by the way. We remember one from Buena Vista that was nearly nine years old and very much at its peak.

PINOT BLANC
[Pee-no´ Blon]

Pinot Blanc is considered one of Chardonnay's poor cousins since it is also a white Burgundy grape. Their mutual relation, the white Gamay Beaujolais or Aligoté grape, is apparently neglected altogether in California. The Pinot Blanc itself is more often used in the *cuvée* for Champagne or blended into the better California Chablis than sold under its own name. This is rather a mystery, for in the Jesuitical hands of the Novitiate of Los Gatos it becomes quite a fine wine: the kind of tart dry white that's clean and crisp to the taste and boasts a big fruity bouquet. A few wineries can be said to rival the Novitiate for the most remarkable Pinot Blanc each year: Heitz Cellar, Mirassou and Wente Brothers. Surely there must be ground good for growing more of it somewhere within the valleys of Napa, Santa Clara and Livermore where these come from. Raised elsewhere, this grape can produce wine that tastes sometimes too aciditic and occasionally too flat to be considered perfectly balanced. Any greenness should have left the good ones within a year or two of bottling. Pinot Blanc is also produced by: Almadén, Bargetto, Chalone Vineyard, Paul Masson (inconsistently fine) and Pedrizetti.

A really good Pinot Blanc is especially welcome with shellfish; it will go well with fish and chicken and white meats too.

SAUVIGNON BLANC
[So-vee-nyon´ Blon]

This noble variety is not grown abundantly in California. If you've ever tried a dry white from the rainy Graves district just outside Bordeaux, you know what Sauvignon Blanc is—or at least how it tastes when blended with perhaps a third as much Semillon. In sun-kissed California Sauvignon Blanc makes a somewhat different wine, a big rich one that usually leaves a splendid aftertaste. Its varietal aroma is one of the easiest to recognize

among all of California's whites. It can be very dry or moderately sweet, but in either case you'll notice an earthy character and a certain soft spiciness. The driest ones we know are the estate-bottled Concannon version and Robert Mondavi's excellent Fumé Blanc. (Beringer and Louis M. Martini have marketed dry Sauvignon Blanc as Fumé Blanc also—the flavor is more smoky than earthy, as the name indicates.) We prefer these to the Almadén or Wente Brothers dry Sauvignon Blancs. This wine is perhaps at its level best with shellfish, but may be employed like any other white. Beaulieu, Charles Krug and the Christian Brothers produce very good medium-sweet Sauvignon Blancs which take to slightly sweetish foods and fruits.

SEMILLON
[Say-me-yohn´]

There is only one dry Semillon and Wente is its producer. This is a contention we are prepared to uphold even against the winemasters who made all the others we've ever tried: Almadén, Beaulieu, Charles Krug, Concannon, Inglenook, Louis M. Martini, Novitiate of Los Gatos (labelled simply Dry Sauterne) and Parducci. Theirs will be fine wines, you may be fairly certain, but for us Wente's alone has the haunting beauty of a flute heard over still waters. It is not a great wine, certainly, but it nearly is, and that at less than two dollars the bottle! Dry Semillon should be gowned in a color like light-golden flesh. The taste, like the aroma, is sturdy but intricate and somehow suggestive of woods' earth. It profits from a couple years or more aging in the bottle and may be called up for service any time you feel like an exceptional white wine.

There are both sweet and dry wines from this aristocratic Bordeaux vine which is the chief ingredient of French Sauternes. The sweet Semillons we have enjoyed most are the Concannon, Novitiate of Los Gatos and Wente Brothers "château" versions referred to under Sauterne. Almost as fine in its way is the one Beaulieu produces and calls Sweet Sauterne. Christian Brothers' Sweet Sauternes is also a sweet Semillon, but not one we would compare with any of the above. San Martin Hostess Semillon is a medium-dry and thoroughly pleasant wine unlike any other we've tried.

Johannisberg means the "Hill of St. John," a castle-crowned mountain in Germany's Rheingau which Charlemagne is said to have selected as a site for a vineyard. However that may be, it is fairly certain that the Romans had put it to that same use centuries before his time. It was acquired during the French Revolution by William Prince of Orange. Napoleon confiscated the vineyard after the battle of Jena and made a present of it to one of his marshalls named, appropriately enough, Kellermann. Following Waterloo the Emperor of Austria confiscated it in his turn and gave it to his great Chancellor, Prince von Metternich-Winneburg, whose descendants have owned it ever since.

JOHANNISBERG RIESLING
[Yo-hahn´-iss-bearg Rees´-ling]

The white Riesling grape responsible for all the great Rhine and Moselle wines and found in Alsace and elsewhere attains the peak of its perfection in the vineyards of Schloss Johannisberg, and it is no discredit to the Hill of St. John that California's wineries have almost unanimously adopted its name for their white Riesling wines. Johannisberg Riesling does not repudiate its German virtues in California though it produces a markedly different wine: light, fresh, fruity, crisply aciditic and neither sweet nor dry. Its rich flavor is complemented by a pronounced flowery aroma and a tangy, long-lingering aftertaste.

Freemark Abbey, Heitz Cellar, Llords and Elwood, Novitiate of Los Gatos (available at the winery only) and Souverain (magnificent!) have all in one year or another produced Johannisberg Riesling we considered incomparable, even great.

Almadén, Beaulieu ("Beauclair"), Inglenook and Mirassou (the Santa Clara grown) can usually be counted on for vintages which outclass all but the top-ranking Chardonnays and Sauvignon Blancs, in our opinion. Our experience would indicate that Johannisberg Riesling does best in Napa, Santa Clara and San Benito Counties. We can say with certainty that Sonoma, at least, is not ideal for it; none we've ever had from there could compare at all with any brand we've listed. What we've had from Concannon, Charles Krug, Robert Mondavi and Weibel has been less distinguished than these but still fine. This wine is best with delicate gourmet dishes: seafoods (plain, not creamed), poultry, veal and sometimes pork.

SYLVANER
RIESLING
*[Sill-vahn´ -er
Rees´ -ling]*

Germany's "second" grape is supposed (by the French) to have originated somewhere in Germany or Austria. The Germans call it the Franken Riesling, however, and ascribe its origin to Alsace, where it is most widely cultivated. One of our fondest memories involves a bottle of Beaulieu's 1967 Sylvaner, but the wines one remembers best are by no means always great ones and this variety makes no pretention to greatness in California. Some think it's not even a fine wine all that often, but it can be a damned good one: big, delicately colored, harmonious and suave on the tongue. It is a thirst-quencher par excellence. We are particularly fond of Beaulieu, Mirassou and Parducci Sylvaner; Buena Vista and Paul Masson also do well by this grape. All these wines are good or very good—and under the right circumstances may seem fine indeed! There are at least this many more we know and could enumerate if we felt like it. But since none of our lists lay claim to completeness, we'll leave them for you to discover.

Gewürz is the German word for spicy, but the variety seems to have shed most of its spiciness when it left its native Alsace. Californian Gewürztraminer is pleasantly soft but only mildly perfumed as compared to the Alsatian product; all the same, its aroma is unusually flowery and delicate. (Its cousin the Traminer has the same characteristics, but they are less pronounced and the wine less interesting. Charles Krug and Inglenook produce the only Traminers we've tried.)

The Gewürztraminers we like best are light-bodied and have more than a hint of sweetness. They are: Almadén, Buena Vista (Haraszthy Cabinet Wine—our reigning favorite) and Sebastiani. We would rank a good batch from any of these wineries among California's finest white wines. Wait for a warm afternoon and drink one, moderately chilled, either with fruit and cookies or all by itself. If the experience leaves you an unregenerate despiser of sweetish tendencies in your white wines, you may try the fine Gewürztraminers produced by: Charles Krug, Louis M. Martini (exceptionally fine), Mirassou, J. Pedroncelli and Stony Hill. These are generally downright dry and play any white table-wine role admirably. This wine is best drunk within a year or two of bottling.

GEWÜRZTRAMINER
[Ge-wurts-trah-me´-ner]

Grey Riesling is one of the more popular white wines in Northern California but is very little known outside the state. This is no doubt just as well for the demand sometimes exceeds the supply as it is. The true name of this French grape is the Chauché Gris, but in California it produces a rather Riesling-like wine which completely justifies its new cognomen. The wine is fragrant, fairly low in acid and refreshingly clean on the palate. It makes a splendid breakfast wine if you're a late riser jaded by too many Champagne breakfasts. We like it with omelettes and egg dishes, with seafood generally,

GREY RIESLING

and with most of the things that call for good white wines. We favor the Grey Riesling produced in the Livermore Valley by Wente Brothers so much we have little experience to offer in guiding your choice among those of other wineries: Almadén, Beringer, Buena Vista, Charles Krug, Christian Brothers, Inglenook, Korbel, Weibel and Windsor Vineyards.

EMERALD RIESLING

This is a hybrid of Johannisberg Riesling and Muscadelle grapes. It makes a "little" wine, medium dry and pleasing to many but hardly fine. The only two we know about are Paul Masson's Emerald Dry and San Martin's Hostess Emerald Riesling.

CHENIN BLANC
[Sheh-ne´ Blon]

Chenin Blanc is the grape which produces the lovely Vouvray in the central Loire Valley, wherefore it is sometimes called the Pineau de la Loire. California Chenin Blanc is no less lovely and the best ones every year are indubitably among her finest whites. It is a wine which can call up those lines of Swinburne's

Eyes coloured like a water-flower
And deeper than the green sea's glass . . . .

It alternately takes on light-yellow or green tints and can look almost perfectly clear, like water itself. The wine is fruity, soft, medium-dry and frequently memorable; its sweetness exceeds any except sweet Semillon, Sauvignon Blanc and Gewürztraminer wines as a rule. For this reason some may prefer to serve it before or after meals, but it makes an excellent dinner companion with carefully chosen dishes—fish with creamed sauces, for one. This is one California wine we've found to vary noticeably from year to year. Every one of the wine-producing counties has come up with superior vintages at one time or another. To judge from our experience, the most consistently outstanding Chenin Blanc would seem to come from: Almadén, Charles Krug (unforgettable at best!), Christian Brothers and Mirassou (1970 Monterey most noteworthy).

This is only our impression, however, and not intended as disparagement of any other producers of fine Chenin Blanc we've tried and can recommend: Beringer, Chalone Vineyard, Cuvaison, Inglenook, Korbel, Mayacamas, Robert Mondavi, J. Pedroncelli, San Martin, Sebastiani, Souverain, Weibel and Windsor Vineyards.

An almost completely dry Chenin Blanc wine is available from Charles Krug, Inglenook, Louis M. Martini and Parducci. All except Martini call it White Pinot, for reasons we cannot fathom. These are very good in their way but for us lack the finesse and charm of the mellower version.

GREEN HUNGARIAN

Green Hungarian is found only in California. Like the Zinfandel its lineage is obscure, not to say unknown. It makes a very pleasant "little" wine that is usually dry but may sometimes retain traces of sweetness. And, yes, you may detect a greenish cast to its color. A number of wineries use it in their blends for Rhine wine and Chablis and a handful bottle it as a varietal. This is not a noble grape, but the wine it produces has its own distinct charm and few regret making its acquaintance, particularly over a light luncheon. Sebastiani probably produces the best Green Hungarian; the only other winery that can equal theirs is, in our opinion, Buena Vista. Pedrizetti, Souverain and Weibel also offer very creditable wines of this type.

SAUVIGNON VERT
[So-vee-nyon´ Vair]

This is the "other" white grape of Bordeaux. In California it is used in blending *ordinaires*. A friend assures us it can make a fine white and has been bottled as a varietal by Mendocino Vineyards; we have yet to try it.

This is another grape widely used in *ordinaire* and another wine we've never tried. It is available as a varietal from Parducci and Wittwer Winery.

FRENCH COLUMBARD

This is the grape from which Cognac is made. Louis M. Martini is the only California winery producing it as a varietal so far as we know. The one bottle we have tasted we found very tart and acidic but otherwise unremarkable.

FOLLE BLANCHE
[Fohl Blonsch]

Wente Brothers blend this variety with Chenin Blanc to come up with something they label Le Blanc de Blancs. Apparently the aberration of a mad winemaster, this wine is the undisputed winner of our Vilest California Premium White Wine award. Each of our friends who has tried it shared our reaction, so take note.

UGNI BLANC
[Oo´-nyee Blon]

Sauterne is a term that calls for clarification. The tiny Sauternes commune near Bordeaux is world famous for the liquorous, sweet light wine a certain few châteaux produce there. The greatest is acknowledged to be Château d'Yquem. Sauternes is the only place besides Germany's Rheingau and the Tokay district of Hungary where an unappetizing-looking fungus variously known as *pourriture noble, edelfaule* or "the noble rot" will flourish on grapes that are allowed to over-ripen. The fungus lives on the juice of the grape and the sugar content of what remains becomes higher and more concentrated. Those vineyards which can take the trouble to use only bunches or even individually selected grapes that are so affected produce astonishing wine.

SAUTERNE
[So-tair´n]

That Sauterne—spelled without the "S"—has become a generic name for American wines defies explanation. The "noble rot" is not found in this country, though the grapes from which the great Sauternes and other Bordeaux whites are made have made themselves at home in California. Most of the wine sold as Sauterne contains very little of these grapes but some wineries produce premium Sauternes made exclusively from them. Now Semillon and Sauvignon Blanc, the principal white Bordeaux grapes, may be made into dry or sweet wines and the two are frequently blended. The sweetest type is usually made from Semillon only and has the word "château" on the label. (Château Concannon, Château Novitiate and Wente's Château Semillon for instance.) "Haut Sauterne" means much the same thing as "sweet"; but some Sauterne labelled "sweet" is merely medium-dry! Beaulieu's Haut Sauterne and Charles Krug's Sweet Sauternes are examples of what we mean. Beringer, Buena Vista and Korbel are a few of the producers of very good dry Sauterne. All these we've singled out stand hair and eyebrows above most other generically named white wines and make premium Sauterne worth considering separately. This is not to say we find them as distinctive or as interesting as varietal wines made from Semillon or Sauvignon Blanc, whether sweet or dry. Similarities between any of these and a fine French Sauternes are purely imaginary.

PREMIUM GENERIC WHITE WINES

It's generally advisable to buy these wines by the jug instead of by the fifth, for reasons we've gone into elsewhere. The best grapes practically never predominate in the blend for a generic, and what results seldom fails to fall short of fine wine. Nevertheless, Rhine wine and Chablis are bottled and sold as premium wines by most wineries. We've found very few we thought worth their premium prices. Among them we include: Beaulieu, Charles

Krug, Heitz, Korbel, Mirassou, Novitiate of Los Gatos and Windsor Vineyards (Tiburon Vintners).

Few of these wineries make much use of white Burgundy grapes from the Chablis district in this wine, however. Very good Chablis is sold in bulk by such producers as Louis Foppiano and Parducci among others; the wineries we have listed are the only producers of Chablis which has, on the average, outclassed the best bulk brands according to our notes. They are not very consistent, however. "Marrying" the wines in a mixture is a tricky business and any vintner's success will vary from year to year. For example, some of the finest and some of the most ordinary premium California Chablis we've tasted have come from Inglenook. The most outstanding premium Rhine-type wines we remember are Concannon's Livermore Valley Moselle and Buena Vista's Vine Brook.

Rosé is the all-purpose wine that never clashes with the menu; it is always refreshing to drink and ever so pleasing to look at. The fact that Lancer's Portuguese Crackling Rosé is the best-selling imported wine in the United States—and that at a ridiculous price—attests to our national naiveté in matters vinous. It also shows that rosé is the easiest wine for non-wine drinkers to enjoy. Not even varietal rosés are intended to be especially distinctive or very fine wines, but this does not keep them from being delicious. You'll find no great variety of scents and flavors among generic rosés so you may as well buy the cheapest you can find. Varietal rosés, on the other hand, are often good enough to be worth seeking out. The Grenache grape is responsible for most of the better European and Californian rosés. The rosés which the Gamay and Zinfandel yield in California are even better yet. Our favorites are the Zinfandels, which are generally bone dry. Bargétto, Concannon, Mayacamas, Pedrizetti, Pedroncelli, Pesenti and Santa Barbara Winery all make very good Zinfandel rosés.

ROSÉ
[Row-zay´]

Grignolino rosé is a startling orange hue and is very pleasant also. We can recommend Emile's Private Stock Brand and Heitz Cellar's. The most distinguished pink wines we've ever had, however, were made from Cabernet Sauvignon by Buena Vista and Llords and Elwood. Ranking with these is the one which we are told was invented through a happy accident by Mirassou. They call it Petite Rosé from the Petite Sirah that goes into it.

Rosé wines may be light or deep pink, medium or bone dry. They profit not at all from bottle aging; the younger they are drunk the better they seem to be. Ham, in any of its multitudinous preparations is the one dish that may seem absolutely to require rosé as an accompanist, but none will refuse it.

CABERNET
SAUVIGNON
[Ka-bear-nay´
So-vee-nyon´]

This is at best a wine fit to accompany an hour of Pergolese or Mozart. Its character, like their music, is both strong and delicate, infinitely rich in nuance yet completely balanced and harmonious. Cabernet Sauvignon generally starts off a deep ruby color which takes on a tinge of orange with age. Though you will find them of every consistency, the best seem to be neither slender nor especially powerful in build but medium-bodied, in-between. Cabernet Sauvignon is the principal grape producing the master wines of Bordeaux: Lafite-Rothschild, Margaux, Haut-Brion, Latour, Mouton-Rothschild and all those other nobles whose company these keep. In California it is generally acknowledged the most extraordinary of her fine reds. Most of the best comes from Napa and Sonoma, with Santa Clara/Santa Cruz close seconds. In France it is always blended, but Californian Cabernet Sauvignon will stand very little blending without suffering and frequently is not blended at all. What results is a wine that in some respects out-Clarets Bordeaux: in flavor generally more forceful and less complex, but just as warm and richly scented. We were not surprised to find Mr. Hugh Johnson recounting that the director of some great château in the Bordeaux region pronounced Souverain Cellars 1961 Cabernet Sauvignon better than his own wine of that superb year. Like Bordeaux, Cabernet Sauvignon should *never* be drunk immediately; it starts out full of tannin and therefore astringent as anything can be, rough and hard. Only time can transmute such wine into elixir; most will continue to improve for twenty or thirty years if given a good home. Admittedly it is already drinkable at the age of four or five, but by the time it's seven or eight that same wine is something else indeed, and well worth waiting for. (Hopefully all this makes you want to lay away a few cases every year—it's possible to arrange here on earth for certain of those rewards which are in heaven, you know.)

Cabernet Sauvignon can be drunk with any food you think calls for an exceptional red wine. Some like it with ham, though it would not be our first choice in this case. To us, on the other hand, it seems the perfect accompaniment to lamb, a judgment with which many will disagree. Some friends, lunching with someone who didn't like white wines, discovered Cabernet Sauvignon can even enhance seafood admirably. And you can always savor it for its own sweet sake, like the music of a Mozart.

At best, Cabernet Sauvignon is one of the world's great wines. Some of the best we remember drinking came from the following wineries: Beaulieu (most especially the Georges de Latour Private Reserve!), Charles Krug (the "vintage selection" in particular), Cresta Blanca, Heitz Cellar, Inglenook (oftentimes the "cask bottlings"), Llords & Elwood, Louis M. Martini, J. Mathews and Souverain Cellars.

Among wineries that in our view produce almost equally fine though very rarely great Cabernet Sauvignon we include Buena Vista, Concannon, Mayacamas, Mirassou and J. Pedroncelli. Our experience cannot guarantee us or you that any bottle from any of these wineries will be truly great. We have, however, learned we can expect from them what, in the words of the contemporary poet Jack Gilbert, ". . . is the normal excellence, of long accomplishment."

PINOT NOIR
[Pee-no´ Nwor]

Marching past Burgundy's Clos de Vougeot, one of Napoleon's Colonels called his men to attention and ordered them to present arms to the vineyard. *"Mes braves,"* he is reported to have said, "it is to defend beauties like these that you are called upon to fight." The great grape of that vineyard is the Pinot Noir. Burgundies which attain a greatness of their own comparable to the greatest Clarets are rare in France; California Pinot Noirs equal to the best Cabernet Sauvignon do not exist. The best ones can be very fine wines, nevertheless: rich, full-bodied and velvety with an aggressively individual flavor and the color of the wine-dark sea. They profit enormously from a stay of at least two or three years in the bottle, but only a few improve enough to keep as much as five years.

Napa, Sonoma and Santa Clara are generally thought the most successful growing regions, although as a general rule we have found Napa Valley Pinot Noir to be lighter in color and body than might be ideal. The best we ever had, however, was produced nearby at Suisun. It came from Mario Lanza's Wooden Valley Winery and a joy it was. Of the major producers we consider Beringer and Paul Masson as tied for the most consistently mediocre. Perhaps no winery turns out fine Pinot Noir consistently, but the brands we usually buy, hoping for the best, include: Almadén, Beaulieu (especially "Beaumont"), Buena Vista, Hanzell (very frequently fine), Heitz, Korbell, Llords & Elwood, Louis M. Martini (very fine indeed most of the time!), Parducci (not available every year), San Martin, Weibel and Wente Brothers (out of sight "Special Selections"!). Perhaps San Martin and Weibel should be grouped with Christian Brothers, Inglenook and Charles Krug, which, while always good, are to our taste only sometimes worthy of a salute.

PETITE SIRAH
[Puh-teat´ Cyr-ah´]

Petite Sirah may have been growing in the Rhône Valley north of the French Riviera back in the days when Pliny the Elder and Plutarch were singling out the wines of this region for special accolades. But tradition says it was introduced by a returning crusader, the worthy Sir Gaspard de Sterimberg. It's been thought the variety originated around Schiraz, Persia, but any etymological basis for this assumption is shaky since the grape is also known as Sirrac, Serrine and Syrrah. Though the date is variously given—1124 or 1225— it is certain that Sir Gaspard began raising it when he gave up this world for the life of a hermit at St. Christophe's on the mountain which has ever since produced one of the world's great wines, Hermitage. This "manliest of wines," as the blessed Saintsbury called it, consists mainly of Petite Sirah, which is also the backbone of our beloved Chateauneuf-du-Pape.

The grape which boasts this distinguished, if confused, pedigree also produces some of California's least known but most outstanding varietal wines. We are told that two distinct varieties are raised under this name in California. We cannot say whether we should look to this or to the way the wine is made or to the ground the grape is grown on for the differences among Petite Sirah wines. Mendocino's Parducci produces a rich-tasting version that improves hugely with a few years bottle aging. In Sonoma Louis Foppiano produces a Petite Sirah which at four dollars the gallon is probably California's best buy in bulk wines. Windsor Vineyards and Trentadue—also in Sonoma—and Napa's Souverain Cellars offer Petite Sirahs of greater distinction, but for a wine of uncompromising character, so mouth-filling it resembles a pachyderm in body, look to the Concannon Vineyard of Livermore Valley.

Number 1020 of the estate-bottled Concannon 1965 vintage limited bottling of 6576 bottles, which we happen to be drinking at the moment, is not such a wine as will appeal to everybody. It is soft and mellow but very dry, with moderate acidity and superb bouquet.

A harder and more tannic red is Mirassou's Monterey-Santa Clara Petite Sirah, when it's really excellent. There seems to be considerable variance from bottle to bottle every vintage however, and it's less than excellent sometimes.

Like Pinot Noir, Petite Sirah takes to heavier dishes: steaks, roasts, turkey, game or what-have-you.

Barbera is another rich red wine with distinctive flavor and full body. It originated in Northern Italy's Piedmonte, whence it was transplanted to California where it does as well as ever it did in Italy. It ages well: indeed, we have had old Barberas whose bouquet was discernible all around the table as soon as the first glass was poured. They proved on tasting as elegant and harmonious as any fine wine could hope to be. With generally moderate tannin but enough acidity to be quite tart when young, Barbera is a rugged, purple-colored wine whose qualities have been underestimated. It is rightly considered one of Sebastiani's "showpiece" wines. Other excellent Barberas are available from Bargétto, Louis M. Martini and Pedrizetti. Apparently only Italian-owned wineries produce it. It goes well with anything hearty.

BARBERA
[Bar-bear´-ah]

Related is Barberone or "Big Barbera," a considerably rougher and coarser wine which is made just a touch or two sweeter and is usually sold in bulk. We recommend the "CK" brand.

GAMAY or
GAMAY
BEAUJOLAIS
[Gah-may´
Bo-zho-lay´]

These are two very similar varieties. Today nobody seems completely sure which of the two is the genuine grape of Beaujolais from the south of Burgundy. Not that it really matters, for the wines they produce are almost indistinguishable in California, usually "little" with grapy aroma of no particular distinction, light in body and in color and with a pleasant, fruity taste. None of it has the magic of the best French Beaujolais—which are not plentiful anywhere—though like Beaujolais, the younger it is drunk, the better it's likely to be. Gamay or Gamay Beaujolais is best as a picnic or lunch-time wine with stews, chops, fried chicken, omelettes and cold meats. We would not serve it as a dinner wine, however. We prefer it cooler than other reds.

There are between twenty-five and thirty wineries we know of currently producing a Gamay or Gamay Beaujolais, and every one we have tried has ranked as better than *ordinaire* but few are fine. This makes it impossible to distinguish favored growing regions and very difficult to single out favorite brands. Sebastiani produced the hands-down best Gamay Beaujolais of 1968 by our reckoning, but Beaulieu, Robert Mondavi and Paul Masson especially have easily ranked with Sebastiani ever since. Though the quality of each fluctuates, the differences are fairly slight, so you may as well buy the cheapest you can find every year and make that the basis for comparison. In addition to those already mentioned, you have the following.

Gamay: Charles Krug (C. Mondavi & Sons), Christian Brothers, East-Side Winery, Inglenook, Louis M. Martini, Mayacamas, Oakville, Pedrizetti, Sutter Home Winery, Trentadue, Tiburon Vintners and Weibel.

Gamay Beaujolais: Almadén, Assumption Abbey (Brookside Vineyards), Fetzer Vineyards, J. Filippi Vintage, Louis Foppiano, Opici Winery, Parducci, San Antonio Winery, San Martin, Wooden Valley and Weibel.

CHARBONO
[Shar-bo-no']

This is a fairly distinctive, rich and heavy-bodied wine produced from an Italian variety by Inglenook.

ZINFANDEL
[Zin'-fan-dell]

Zinfandel can be all things to all men—almost. In the first place, you're free to make up your very own account of where this variety came from and who sent it to California. The first man to raise it, Colonel Haraszthy, never could solve this puzzle and neither has any one since. Zinfandel is found only in California, where more acreage is devoted to it than to any fine wine grape today. Because it's plentiful and drinkable immediately after fermentation and because it's good, this wine has often been dubbed California's answer to French Beaujolais. This is all true, but it doesn't go far enough, for Zinfandel is also extensively used to produce rosé and is a major ingredient in many blends for California Claret. Ridge Vineyards has even introduced an excellent sweet dessert wine called Zinfandel Essence. Also, of course, it is our bulk varietal wine, seldom any more expensive than a generic *ordinaire* and usually several cuts higher in quality.

Zinfandel has an especially fruity aroma to it and is generally light-bodied and smooth. In color it is—well—neither so dark as some reds nor so light as some others. The flavor may strike you as raspberry-like somehow, but you're sure to find it zesty. Zinfandel thrives throughout California, but apparently it finds itself most at home in the cooler north coastal counties. Some of the wine made from it in hot regions of the state is utterly unlike our description but downright unpleasant in its own right. D'Agostini, however, also produces a weird version in mountainous Amador County. It's always interesting to come across a Zinfandel that has gained in stature as a result of a few years in the bottle. The very best ones can become fine, distinctive wine with a little time. Occasionally fine, sometimes *ordinaire,* and mostly plain good wine—there's a Zinfandel of some sort for just about any menu that demands red wine. You may feel that such light reds as this are happiest setting off chicken or pasta dishes or possibly serving as the color guard beside light meats or omelettes.

It pleases us to think that some of the finest Zinfandel available still comes from the same winery where it was first produced, Haraszthy's Buena Vista. Our other favorites at present are Charles Krug, Christian Brothers generally, Louis Martini especially, Mirassou and also Ridge. A few years back we should have included Inglenook and probably San Martin among the producers of fine Zinfandel. They remain very good certainly, but for whatever reason they now fall somewhat short of fine we think. Along with these, some other brands of Zinfandel which have impressed us as being well above average must include Almadén, Heitz Cellar, Parducci, Sebastiani and Simi. No doubt there are others we don't know either enough or anything about which deserve to be included.

PINOT SAINT GEORGES *[Pee-no′ Sein Zhorge]*

This is not a true Pinot. It is a light wine of no distinction which is deservedly obscure. Inglenook sometimes and Christian Brothers regularly produce it. This is also known as Red Pinot.

GRIGNOLINO *[Greeg-no-lee′-no]*

This grape is another native of Italy's Piedmonte which is bottled as a varietal by Beringer, Heitz and San Martin in California. This "little" wine has a peculiar orange-red color and a very pleasant fragrance.

RUBY CABERNET

A few wineries market something called simply "Cabernet" which we assume to mean Ruby Cabernet, a hybrid of greater yield but considerably less distinguished character than its mother variety, Cabernet Sauvignon.

167

PREMIUM GENERIC RED WINES

We generally buy California Burgundy, Claret and Chianti by the jug, since these are practically never fine wines. They range from the very bad to the very good. Only a very few among the premium generics are sufficiently superior to the best of the "sound standard" versions to be worth the extra expensé. We shall merely supplement what we have said elsewhere about generic wines by citing those few here. Buena Vista, Mirassou and Wente Burgundies usually seem a little better to us than Charles Krug, Christian Brothers, San Martin and Souverain—our other favorites. This is the consensus of our cellar books, but there can be wide variations between one batch and another of any producer's blended generic wines. All we can safely say, therefore, is that these are about the only ones we know of which we would prefer to the best bulk Burgundies, Cambiaso Vintners Reserve or Mondavi Vintage for example. We think the Clarets produced by Charles Krug, Christian Broathers and Louis M. Martini and the Chiantis coming from San Martin and Sebastiani are worth their premium prices.

It is not too much to hope that generic names are gradually falling into disuse. Almost every winery still markets something or other called Burgundy, but the names Claret and Chianti are much less widely used than they were ten years ago. A very successful wine in this class which is as good as any we have mentioned is marketed by Paul Masson under the proprietary name "Rubion." Beringer has a beautiful blend of Grignolino and Pinot Noir called "Barenblut." As the public becomes more knowledgeable perhaps the better wineries will stop selling their blends under names that make them look like self-confessed but unsuccessful imitations of foreign products.

WINE GLOSSARY
What does that mean?

Thus I write to thee in balmy peace, and tell thee trivial things scarce worthy ink.

Charles Reade

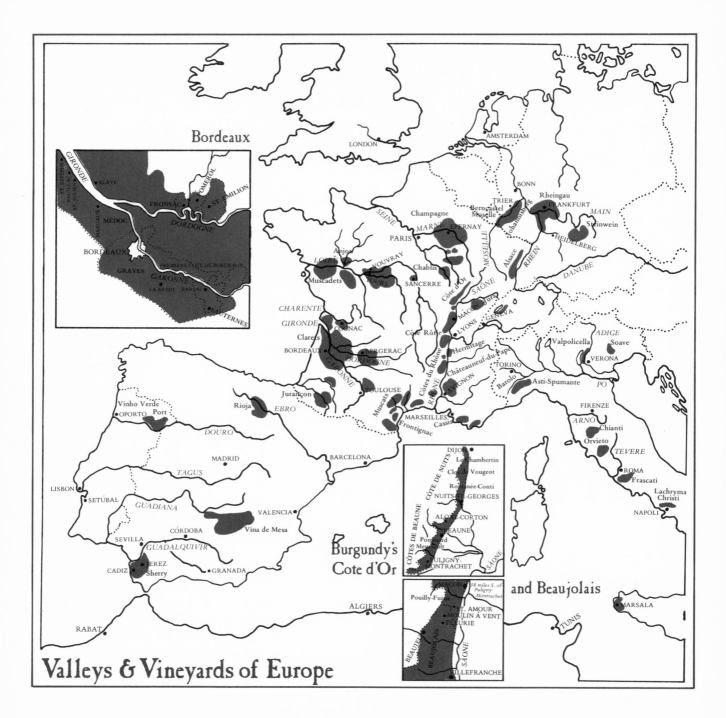

Bordeaux

GIRONDE

ST. ESTÈPHE
PAUILLAC
ST. JULIEN
BLAYE
MARGAUX
MÉDOC
FRONSAC
ST. EMILION
DORDOGNE
POMEROL
BORDEAUX
GRAVES
PREMIÈRE CÔTE DE BORDEAUX
GARONNE
LA BRÈDE
BARSAC
SAUTERNES

LONDON
AMSTERDAM
BONN
TRIER
Rheingau
FRANKFURT
MAIN
Champagne
Berncastel
Moselle
Johannisberg
Steinwein
MARNE
EPERNAY
HEIDELBERG
PARIS
Alsace
RHEIN
SEINE
Anjou
VOUVRAY
Chablis
Côte d'Or
MOSELLE
LOIRE
TOURS
SANCERRE
SAONE
Muscadets
Mâcon
Jura
Côte Rôtie
LYONS
GENEVA
ADIGE
CHARENTE
Valpolicella
Soave
GIRONDE
COGNAC
Hermitage
VERONA
Clarets
BERGERAC
Châteauneuf-du-Pape
BORDEAUX
DORDOGNE
AVIGNON
TORINO
GARONNE
Barolo
Asti-Spumante
PO
TOULOUSE
FIRENZE
Jurançon
Muscats
ARNO
Vinho Verde
Rioja
EBRO
Frontignac
Cassis
Chianti
OPORTO
Port
MARSEILLES
Orvieto
TEVERE
DOURO
BARCELONA
ROMA
MADRID
Frascati
TAGUS
Lachryma
Christi
LISBON
NAPOLI
SETÚBAL
GUADIANA
Vina de Mesa
VALENCIA
CÓRDOBA
SEVILLA
GUADALQUIVIR
JEREZ
Sherry
CADIZ
GRANADA
ALGIERS
MARSALA
RABAT
TUNIS

Burgundy's Cote d'Or

DIJON
Le Chambertin
Clos de Vougeot
CÔTE DE NUITS
Romanée-Conti
NUITS-ST.-GEORGES
ALOXE-CORTON
CÔTES DE BEAUNE
BEAUNE
Pommard
Meursault
SAONE
PULIGNY-MONTRACHET

and Beaujolais

MÂCON
38 miles S. of Puligny-Montrachet
Pouilly-Fuissé
ST. AMOUR
MOULIN À VENT
FLEURIE
BEAUJEU
BEAUJOLAIS
SAONE
VILLEFRANCHE

Valleys & Vineyards of Europe

ACIDITY
Fixed acidity is the wine's natural fruit-acid content which can only be determined by tasting. Volatile acidity is the vinegar or acetic-acid content of a wine and is detectable in the smell; no good wine has more that a trace of it.

ALAMEDA
California winegrowing county due east of San Francisco which includes the Livermore Valley, famous for excellent white wines.

AMONTILLADO [Ah-mont-ee-ah´-doe]
Popular type of Sherry, very dry and usually well aged. Spanish.

APÉRITIF [Ah-pear-ee-teef´]
An appetizer, usually a flavored and/or fortified wine. (French)

ANGELICA
A sweet fortified wine apparently invented in Southern California and named after the City of the Angels; worth knowing in order to avoid.

APPELLATION CONTRÔLÉE
[Ah´-pell-ah-see-ohn Cawn-trol-ay´]
French. Literally "controlled appellation." Words found on the label of any genuine French wine of real quality guaranteeing that it is entitled to the name it bears. The finer the wine, the more specific the designation. Names of vineyards, villages, communes, and whole districts are officially recognized and delimited.

ARMAGNAC [Ar-mahn-nyack´]
Region in France near the Pyrenees which produces a splendid brandy of the same name.

AROMA
The distinctive odor of the particular grape from which the wine was made.

ASTI SPUMANTE
[Ahs-tee´ Spoo-mahn´-tay]
Italian sparkling wine from the Piedmont region.

ASTRINGENCY
Wines that seem to dry and pucker the mouth and feel rough on the tongue are astringent. This is usually due to excessive tannin and tends to disappear with bottle-aging.

AUSLESE *[Ows´-lay-seh]*
Literally "selected"; indicates the wine is from the ripest selected bunches of grapes which have the *edelfaule* or "noble rot" on them. See *edelfaule*.

BAROLO *[Bah-roh´-low]*
An excellent Italian red wine from the Piedmont region.

BARSAC *[Bar-sok´]*
Wine from the commune of this name in the Sauternes district near Bordeaux; sweet, but generally drier than Sauternes.

BEAUNE *[Bone]*
A winemaking and marketing center for Burgundy's wines located in the Côte de Beaune (the southern section of the Côte d'Or).

BEERENAUSLESE *[Beer´-en-ows´-lay-seh]*
German. Literally "berry-selected." Rich, sweet and expensive wine made from individually selected grapes which are over-ripe and covered with the "noble rot."

BERGERAC *[Bear´-zhair-ack´]*
Bergerac wine named for the town near Bordeaux; dry reds and semi-sweet whites, both very good as a rule.

BERNCASTEL *[Burn´-kass-tell]*
Small town on the Moselle which produces very fine wines, Berncasteler Doktor being the most famous.

BLANC DE BLANC *[Blon deh Blon]*
White wine from white grapes, especially Champagnes (which are customarily made from both white and black grapes).

BOCKSBEUTEL *[Box´-boy-tell]*
German. The squat flagon in which white Steinwein from Germany and Chilean Riesling is bottled.

BODEGA *[Bo-day´-gah]*
Spanish. A winery, a wine shop or a wine producer's cellars, usually above ground.

BODY
The density or consistency of a wine in relation to its alcoholic strength.

BOTTLE SICKNESS
A kind of claustrophobia that besets most wines after they are first bottled and thus deprived of air, resulting in a temporary loss of flavor. It usually lasts only a few weeks but may recur in fine wines after traveling.

BOUQUET *[Boo-kay´]*
French. The scent, the breath a wine gives off in the glass after it is poured. Unlike aroma, bouquet is produced by bottle aging.

BOURGOGNE *[Boor-goyn´]*
French name for the province of Burgundy.

BREED
The total virtues of a wine, considering all the qualities associated with that type of wine.

BRUT *[Brewt]*
French. Literally "unmodified"; applies to very dry Champagnes to which little or no *dosage* has been added.

CABINET or KABINETT) *[Kah-be-net´]*
A superior grade of German wine. Use of this term, however, has been so loose that a Kabinett-wein today is often nothing special.

CALVADOS *[Kal-vah-doz´]*
Applejack brandy from the French province of Normandy.

CAVES *[Kahv]*
French. Literally "Cellars," wine storehouses.

CHABLIS *[Shahb-lee´]*
A white-wine region of northern Burgundy, producing fine wines exclusively from Pinot Chardonnay. Petit Chablis is only slightly less fine than the "grand cru" appellation.

CHAMBERTIN *[Shawm-bear-tehn´]*
Classic Burgundy red-wine vineyard, name also given to village and commune of Gevrey-Chambertin. "Le Chambertin" is the best of several Burgundies, legally allowed to use this name in hyphenated form.

CHAMBRER *[Shawm-bray´]*
French. To bring a wine to room temperature.

CHARMAT BULK PROCESS
A shortcut method of making sparkling wine invented by the Frenchman Charmat. It produces inferior bubbly.

CHIANTI *[Key-ahn´tee]*
An Italian wine named for the region in central Italy.

CLARET

The common English name for the red wines of Bordeaux. These were originally called *vin clairet*, or "clear wine," to distinguish them from the wine which was kept in cellars to mature. *Vin clairet* was primarily used for export.

CLOS *[Klo]*

French. Literally, an enclosed yard; vineyard, usually of high repute.

COGNAC *[Ko´-nyack]*

French Brandy from the district it's named for.

COMMUNE *[Koh-mewh´]*

French. A parish or township.

CONTRA COSTA

Wine-producing county of California that lies north of Alameda and east of Napa. Its red wines are its finest.

CORTON-CHARLEMAGNE
[Kohr´ -tohn scharl´ h'mahn]

Classic Burgundy vineyard producing both red wine and white.

CÔTE (-S) *[Coat]*

French. Literally "slope" or "hillside"; a winegrowing area.

CÔTE D'OR *[Coat dohr´]*

A region of central Burgundy, some thirty-six miles long and less than one mile wide, where the finest Burgundies are grown.

CÔTE RÔTIE *[Coat Row-tee´]*

A red-wine region on the Rhône near Vienne producing fine reds.

CRACKLING

Semi-sparkling, slightly fizzy. "Pétillant."

CRU *[Crew]*

French. Literally a "growth," a planting or crop; a vineyard or group of vineyards; wine from a specific vineyard.

CRUST

The sediment that adheres to the inside of a bottle, indicating a well-aged wine. Especially "crusted" vintage Port.

CUVÉE *[Koo-vay´]*

French. Literally "tubful"; the blend of several wines, as for Champagne.

DEMI-SEC
French. Fairly sweet. Usually used to describe sparkling wines.

DESSERT WINES
Sweet wines served either with dessert or as dessert themselves, alone. Generally fortified.

DOMAINE *[Doe-main´]*
French. Vineyard. The control or management of several vineyards.

DOSAGE *[Doe-saaje´]*
French. The process of adding sugared wine and brandy to bottle-fermented sparkling wines before they are corked.

DOURO *[Door´-roh]*
A river and a wine region of central Portugal famous for Port.

DOUX *[Doo]*
French. Sweet.

D'YQUEM (CHÂTEAU) *[Dee-kem´]*
"First growth" Sauternes, Bordeaux.

EAUX-DE-VIE *[Oh-deh-vee´]*
French. Brandy distilled from the leavings of crushed grapes, usually raw and terrifyingly powerful. Same as *marc* or *grappa*.

EDELFAULE *[Ay´-dell-fohl]*
German. The so-called 'noble rot' or *pourriture noble; Botrytis cinerea,* a type of mold which forms on overripe white grapes in certain Rhine districts and in Sauternes which is responsible for their sweetest and finest white wines.

ENOLOGY
The science and study of making wine and growing grapes for wine, pioneered by Louis Pasteur; it is related to viticulture.

ESTATE-BOTTLED
Semi-official designation of a wine fermented and bottled on the specific vineyard property where the grapes were grown. California's equivalent to "château-bottled," etc.

FEINSTE *[Fine´-st]*
German. The finest, the most excellent. Usually a trustworthy designation on German labels.

FINESSE *[Fee-ness´]*
French. A wine's elegance or delicacy. Also the quality of its aftertaste, the lingering scent and warmth in the throat after a wine has been swallowed.

FINISH
The characteristics of a wine that remain in the mouth and nasal passages after the wine has been swallowed; another term for aftertaste.

FINO [Fee´-no]
Spanish A common type of Sherry, very dry and pale.

FIRMNESS
The rawness typical of young wines, mainly alcoholic in character.

FLOR [Floor]
Spanish. The yeast which is responsible for the nutty character of dry Spanish Sherries. The process is only occasionally used in California.

FORTIFIED WINE
Aperitifs and dessert wines to which grape spirits (brandy) have been added.

FRAPPÉ [Frah-pay´]
French. Iced or chilled.

FRASCATI [Frahs-kaht´-ee]
Best known of Italy's Castelli Romani wines grown near Rome; dry and full-bodied whites and reds.

GENERIC
Names such as Burgundy, Rhine wine, Chianti and so forth as applied to American wines. Used thus without any geographical significance, these names mean next to nothing to the consumer.

GRAND [Grahn]
French. Large, great or superior. Usually, however, unofficial.

GRAPPA [Grah´-pah]
Italian. Distilled grape spirits. (See marc).

GRAVES [Grahv]
An important red and white wine district near Bordeaux.

HARD
Containing too much tannin, hence unpleasant. Such wines, though requiring longer to mature than others, finally lose this hard quality in the process of maturing and become excellent.

HAUT-BRION (CHÂTEAU–)
[Oh-bree-yohn´]
A "First Growth" red Graves considered one of the finest of all Clarets.

HAUT-SAUTERNE *[Oh-so-tairn´]*
An American term for distinguishing sweeter whites, thought to resemble the wines from the Sauternes district in France, from dry Sauterne. The name of the wine, like the name of the district, is always spelled with a final "s" in France, where "dry Sauterne" is unknown.

JOHANNISBERG (SCHLOSS)
[Schlohs Yo-hahn´-iss-bearg]
A world-renowned vineyard on the mountain overhanging Johannisberg in Germany's Rheingau region. It has given its name to the white Riesling grape from which its wines are made.

JURA *[Zhu-rah´]*
Mountainous region of France near the Swiss border which produces red, white and sparkling wines; Arbois and Château Chalon are probably the best known.

JURANÇON *[Zhu-rah-sohn´]*
A full-bodied and usually sweetish white wine of some quality from the region of this name near the Pyrenees in France.

KELLER *[Kell´-er]*
German. Cellar.

KELLER-ABFÜLLUNG
[Kell´-er-Ahb-fuel´ung]
German. Estate-bottled. Equivalent to the French *Mis en bouteilles au domaine* Another term, *Kellerabzug,* has the same meaning. Both indicate that the wine was grown and produced at the particular vineyard specified.

LACHRHYMA CHRISTI
[Lah´ cream-ah Krees´-tee]
Wine from the slopes of Vesuvius. Also a generic term for Italian sparkling wine.

LAFITE-ROTHSCHILD (CHÂTEAU–)
[Lah-feet´ Rote-shield´]
"First Growth" Médoc (Bordeaux), known for great red wines; soft, full-bodied and unbelievable.

LATOUR (CHÂTEAU–) *[Lah-toor´]*
"First Growth" Médoc (Bordeaux), also famous for top-ranking Clarets.

LIQUEUR *[Lee-cur´]*
A sweet cordial or after-dinner drink.

LIVERMORE
See Alameda.

MÂCONNAIS *[Mah-kawn´-ay]*
A wine region of Burgundy, south of the Côte d'Or and north of the Beaujolais; the reds are usually sold as "Bourgogne" or "Mâcon."

MADERISÉ *[Mad-air-ee´-zay]*
French. Literally "like Madeira"; term applied to white wine kept past its prime which has turned brown and usually tastes bad.

MAGNUM
A bottle size twice that of the ordinary bottle, or about two-fifths of a gallon. The Jeroboam, a double magnum with a capacity up to 8-1/2 pints, is the largest.

MANZANILLA *[Mahn-tha-nee´-yah]*
A Sherry-like Spanish wine made in the Sherry country.

MARC *[Mar]*
French. Brandy distilled from the leavings of pressed grapes, sometimes from the must.

MARGAUX *[Mar-goe´]*
A commune of Médoc in the Bordeaux region, named for a great 'First Growth' château located there.

MARQUE DÉPOSÉE *[Mark dey´-poe-zay´]*
French. A registered brand name or trademark.

MARSALA *[Mar-sa´-la]*
A sweetish fortified wine from Sicily, first produced for the English market during the Napoleonic period.

MATEUS *[Maht-ay´-oos]*
A Portuguese rosé from the Douro region.

MAVRODAPHNE *[Mav´-row-daf´-nee]*
A sweet red fortified wine from Greece, often excellent.

MAY WINE
Any light German wine to which the aromatic leaves of the herb *waldmeister* (woodruff) have been added. It is traditionally served cold from a bowl with strawberries floating in it.

MÉDOC *[Meh-dahk´]*
The district in the Bordeaux area which is home to most of the officially classified great Clarets. It produces red wines almost exclusively and includes the communes of Pauillac, Margaux, St. Julien, St. Estèphe, St. Laurent and Macau.

MÉTHODE CHAMPENOISE
[May´-toad shawm-pnwas´]
French. Traditional French process for making Champagne.

MEURSAULT [Mer-so´]
One of the Côte de Beaune communes of Burgundy which produces a top-ranking white wine, dry yet very rich, made exclusively from Pinot Chardonnay.

MISE EN BOUTEILLES AU CHÂTEAU
[Mees´-an-boo-tay´-eh oh-Shah-toe´]
French. Literally "château-bottled." "Mise du Château" or "Mise au Domaine" mean the same thing: that the wine was bottled at the vineyard by the grower. It does not necessarily follow that the wine bottled there was any good.

MONOPOLE [Mon-o-pole´]
French. A monopoly on a brand name, vineyard, or wine.

MONTRACHET [Mown-rash-ay´]
Some of the world's greatest white wine is made from Pinot Chardonnay grown in the Burgundy commune Puligny-Montrachet. (Chassagne-Montrachet grows Pinot Blanc.) The best appellations are Le Montrachet, Chevalier-Montrachet, Batard-Montrachet, Les Bienvenues, Les Criots, and Les Chalumeaux.

MOULIN-A-VENT [Moo´-lan-ah-Vahn]
One of the principal communes of Beaujolais and the name of an outstanding vineyard, home of the very best of Beaujolais, very hearty.

MOUSSEUX [Moos-soh´]
French. Literally "foaming." Any French sparkling wine other than Champagne made by the méthode champenoise.

MOUTON-ROTHSCHILD (CHÂTEAU—)
[Moo-tohn-Rote-shield´]
"Second Growth" Médoc (Bordeaux) producing red wine of greatness. A de facto "première cru."—illustrating the fallibility of the Classification of 1855.

NAPA
(American Indian word for plenty) A valley and county north of the San Francisco Bay famous for some of North America's great Cabernet Sauvignon and fine reds and whites generally. The valley is about thirty-five miles long; its greatest width is about five miles.

NATURE *[Nah-tewr´]*
French. Unsweetened. Virtually the same meaning as *brut,* denoting the driest sparkling wines.

NEW YORK STATE
The second wine-producing state after California. Its foremost vineyards are concentrated in the Finger Lakes region and around Naples, New York. A full line of New York State wines is made from native American grapes. They have a characteristic "foxy" or "wild-grape" flavor which is often offset by blending with California wines. The sparkling and dry white table wines and rosés are considered the district's best. A small quantity of wine also comes from around Highland in the Hudson River Valley and from Rockland County further south.

NOSE
Scent, odor. "A good nose" means a fine bouquet.

NUITS-ST.-GEORGES *[Nwee-san-Jhorge´]*
Wine from the commune and principal town of Burgundy's Côte de Nuits (the northern section of the Côte d'Or which produces many of the world's finest red Burgundies). Especially Les St. Georges, Les Porrets, and Les Pruliers.

OEIL-DE-PERDRIX *[Oye´-deh-pair-dree]*
French. Literally "partridge eye." A traditional term for rosé.

OLOROSO *[Oh-low-row´-so]*
A sweet Spanish Sherry, full-bodied yet delicate.

ORIGINAL ABFULLÜNG
[O-rig´-in-ahl Ahb-fuel´-ung]
Literally "Original bottling." This indicates the wine was grown, fermented and bottled at the vineyard by the owners. (German)

ORVIETO *[Or-vee-ay´-toe]*
A fine Italian white wine from the district of Umbria.

PÉTILLANT *[Pet´-ee-ahn]*
French. Slightly sparkling, fizzy. "Crackling."

PIESPORTER *[Pees´-porter]*
Wines grown in the neighborhood of Piesport, some of the very finest Moselles. Piesporter Goldtropfchen is especially famous.

POMACE

Grape skins, pips and sometimes stems left over after pressing out the must. Brandy is sometimes distilled from it, but it is usually used as fertilizer in the vineyards.

POMMARD *[Poe-mar´]*

A Burgundy commune, Côte de Beaune, famous for soft, delicate, smooth red wines.

POUILLY-FUISSÉ *[Poo´-ee Fwee-Say´]*

An excellent white from one of half a dozen villages in the Mâcon area of southern Burgundy. One of the best-value French wines.

POURRITURE NOBLE

[Poo´-ee-tur´ Nobl]

French. Literally "noble rot." Same as *edelfaule.*

RESERVA *[Ray-zer´-vah]*

Spanish. "Reserve," specially aged.

RETSINA *[Rhet-see´-nah]*

Wine with a turpentiney, resinous taste invented by the ancient Greeks. They did not, as is popularly supposed, first start putting pine resin in their wine to keep the Turks from drinking it.

RHEINGAU *[Rhine´-gow]*

A district along the right bank of the Rhine in Germany, eighteen or twenty miles long and only a few miles across at its widest points. From these southward facing vineyards come some of the world's greatest white wines. Rudesheimer, Geisenheimer, Hattenheimer, Schloss Johannisberg, Erbacher, Eltviller and Hochheimer are only a few of the most highly regarded names.

RHENISH

English term for Rhine wines in Shakespeare's day, later eclipsed by "hock."

RICHEBOURG *[Reesh´-boor]*

A Burgundy vineyard; part of the Romanée "group" of the Côte de Nuits which produces some of the world's most magnificent red wines.

RIOJA *[Ree-oh´-ha]*

District in the Ebro River Valley of Northern Spain which produces excellent red and white wines. Red Rioja Reservas probably represent the best quality for the money available on the world's wine market today.

ROMANEÉ-CONTI
[Row´-mahn-ay´-Kawn´ tee]
A celebrated vineyard in Burgundy's Côte de Nuits, adjoining La Romanée and considered to produce the greatest of red Burgundy wines.

SACK
Term for Sherry current in Shakespeare's day (Falstaff was a sack-addict). The origin of the word is variously explained.

SAN BENITO
California winegrowing county just north of Monterey and south of Santa Cruz which includes what is probably the world's largest vineyard at Paicines.

SANCERRE *[Sahn-sair´]*
A superior white grown in the upper Loire Valley in France and characterized by a beautifully flinty quality. Hemingway's favorite.

SANTA CLARA
A California county south of San Francisco noted for the excellence of its wine, especially that from the Santa Cruz Mountains around Saratoga and Los Gatos.

SANTA CRUZ
A wine-producing county in California which adjoins Santa Clara on the west along the ridge of the Santa Cruz Mountains.

SEKT *[Secht]*
Any German sparkling wine made by the *methode champenoise.*

SOLERA *[Sol´-air-ah]*
Spanish. A series of casks arranged in tiers for aging and blending Sherry. In a Sherry bodega, the contents of each cask are methodically withdrawn and replenished so that the oldest blends are in the last casks from which the finished Sherry comes.

SONOMA
A leading county in the production of superior California wines, especially reds. It is bounded on the east by Napa County, the Mayacamas Mountains forming the intervening border.

SPÄTLESE *[Schpayt´-lay-seh]*
German. Literally "late selection." Wine made from fully-ripened grapes; often indicates some sweetness.

SPRITZIG *[Sprit´-zik]*
German. Semi-sparkling, prickly. "Pétillant."

SYBARITE
A refined voluptuary spiritually akin to the inhabitants of the ancient Greek colony of Sybaris, all of whom were legendary wine bibbers. A good word to know.

TAVEL *[Tah-vell´]*
A commune in the Rhône valley not far from Avignon, producing a fairly dry rosé considered among the best in France.

TERROIR *[tehr-wahr´]*
Literally "ground." The special and unique quality with which a given piece of ground imbues a wine is called the *"goût du terroir."* (French)

TOKAY *[Tow-kay´]*
A celebrated sweet white wine from Tokay, Hungary; California's cheap fortified wine with this name bears no relation to it.

TROCKENBEERENAUSLESE
[Trock´-en-bear´-en-ows´-lay-seh]
German. Literally "individually selected dried berries." Rare, sweet and expensive wine only made in exceptional years, from raisined *edelfaule*-covered grapes.

VARIETAL
A wine named for the grape from which it is made (providing, under California law, that grape makes up at least 51 percent of the wine). In Europe only Alsatian and Italian wines are known by the names of their grapes.

VERMOUTH
A blended wine which is fortified and infused with aromatic herbs and spices. Vermouths may be dark and sweet or light and dry. Both kinds are generally lighter and drier if made in France rather than in Italy. California also produces some very good vermouths. The name is thought to come from the German word *Wermuth*, which means wormwood.

VIN DU PAYS *[Vahn-due-pay-ee]*
French. A term for the local wine of the region, which is rarely marketed outside it.

VITIS LABRUSCA
[Wee´ tiss Lah-brus´-kah]
Latin. Species of grapes native to North America, cultivated and hybridized throughout the Eastern United States. "Fox-grapes."

VITIS VINIFERA
[Wee´-tiss Weh-nif-err´-ah]
Latin. Literally "the winebearer vine." Dominant species of wine grapes native to Europe, now widely grown elsewhere as well.

VOLLRADS (SCHLOSS)
[Schlohs Fahl´-rahdz]
One of the greatest Rheingau vineyards producing wines with a magnificent flowery flavor.

VOUGEOT (CLOS DE—)
[Klo-deh-voo-jhoh´]
A classic vineyard in the Côte de Nuits, renowned for its great red Burgundy.

VOUVRAY *[Voo´-vray]*
A white wine from this region of the central Loire near Tours; unfailingly soft, fruity and pleasant. Excellent sparkling Vouvray is also made.

BIBLIOGRAPHY

The following books were consulted in the course of writing ours:

Adams, Leon D. *The Commonsense Book of Wine.* 1958. David McKay Company, New York.

Allen, H. Warner. *A Contemplation of Wine.* 1951. Michael Joseph, Ltd., London.

Amerine, Maynard A. and Singleton, V. L. *Wine: An Introduction for Americans.* 1965. University of California Press, Berkeley.

Balzer, Robert L. *California's Best Wines.* 1948. Ward Richie Press, Los Angeles.

Belloc, Hilaire. *Advice.* 1960. Harvill Press, London.

Blumberg, Robert S. and Hannum, Hurst. *The Fine Wines of California.* 1971. Doubleday and Company, Garden City.

Churchill, Creighton. *The World of Wines.* 1967. Collier Books, New York.

Grossman, Harold J. *Grossman's Guide to Wine, Spirits and Beers.* 1964. Charles Scribner's Sons, New York.

Haraszthy, Agoston. *Grape Culture, Wines and Wine-making, with Notes upon Horti-culture.* 1862. Harper and Brothers, New York.

Johnson, Hugh. *Wine.* 1967. Simon and Schuster, New York.

Jones, Idwal. *Vines in the Sun.* 1949. William Morrow and Company, New York.

Kressmann, Edouard. *The Wonder of Wine.* 1968. Hastings House, New York.

Lichine, Alexis. *Wines of France.* 1969. Alfred Knopf, New York.

Melville, John. *Guide to California Wines,* Third edition revised by Jefferson Morgan, 1968. Nourse, San Carlos.

Saintsbury, George. *Notes on a Cellar-book.* 1933. Macmillan, New York.

Schoonmaker, Frank and Marvel, Tom. *The Complete Wine Book.* 1934. Simon and Schuster, New York.

Seltman, Charles. *Wine in the Ancient World.* 1957. Routledge and Kegan Paul Company, London.

Sichel, Allan et al. *A Guide to Good Wine.* 1952. W. & R. Chambers, Ltd., London and Edinburgh.

Simon, André L. *Champagne.* 1962. McGraw-Hill, New York.

INDEX

This book is printed on
100 percent recycled paper.
Recycle your wine bottles, too.

BIOGRAPHICAL NOTES

The first member of his family to live outside the South, James Norwood Pratt was brought up believing the first duty of a wine is to be red. He was educated at the University of North Carolina and abroad, but it was not until he adopted San Francisco in 1965 that he undertook a systematic exploration of the world of wine. He is a known lover of poetry, a classics scholar and a practicing alchemist.

Jacques de Caso initiated the cataloging of Baron Philippe de Rothschild's collection of art and *objets* relating to wine which is now housed in the Musée du Vin at Château Mouton-Rothschild, Pauillac, France. He is now a citizen of the United States and professor of the history of art at the University of California at Berkeley. The two of them first met early in 1970 and discovered a remarkable coincidence of tastes and interest in wine and other things which has resulted in the present volume. Between them they have now consumed over three thousand bottles of California wine, Norwood Pratt says, "by conservative estimates."

Sara Raffetto studied art at the University of California at Berkeley and later in Los Angeles with Rico LeBrun. She was awarded a Fulbright in 1961 to study painting in Italy. Her work is represented in Boston's De Cordova Museum and in numerous private collections.